The Smart

MW01242153

How to Stop Living
Paycheck to Paycheck

Second Edition

by Avery Breyer

A note from the author: Personally, I'd rather leave things to common sense, good ethics, and everyone having a sense of personal responsibility for their actions. And like any decent person should do, obviously I do my best to provide accurate information at all times. But the experts say it's better to put proper disclaimers in place, so here goes...

READ THIS FIRST!

Just to say thanks for downloading my book, I'd like to give you **my FREE special report, How to Save Money When You Don't Have Any.**

I think you'll find it interesting -- it contains a really simple savings strategy that most people overlook.

I'll also give you **a FREE copy of the Money Tracker.** This is an insanely useful tool that I've used for years to keep an eye on my budget. I can tell you from personal experience that using my Money Tracker is far easier than making your own from scratch, or using an old-fashioned notebook to keep tabs on your budget!

Ready?

Get it all here:

https://averybreyer.com/1hr-budget-how-to-stop-living-paycheck-to-paycheck-opt-in/

Contents

Introduction

Welcome to the Smart Money Blueprint: How to Stop Living Paycheck to Paycheck!

Do you want to learn proven techniques that will help you to stop living paycheck to paycheck and stop stressing out about money?

Do you want to be able to relax, knowing that all of your needs, today and in the future, can be paid for with ease?

Look, we've all gone through tough times with money, but the good news is that it doesn't have to be that way.

Maybe credit card debt is the only way you are able to keep afloat right now, although you know that's not a long-term solution. Maybe you feel ashamed that you're not doing a better job of managing your money — you feel frustrated that you can't get ahead. And maybe you've tried budgeting, but it just didn't work for you.

This book is going to show you solutions that actually work.

This book will provide you with both the tools and the knowledge that you need to finally get ahead.

You'll learn a step-by-step system that is easy to implement, and takes only one hour a month to maintain (15 minutes once per week). I promise you that if you read this book and follow the advice in here, you'll be set on a path to a world where you control your money, you have a plan that will ensure you don't run out of money, and you are no longer a slave to your bills.

Stand up to your obstacles and do something about them. You will find that they haven't half the strength you think they have.

Why I Wrote This Book

It kills me to see people in financial trouble, when they could have easily avoided it if only they'd had the tools and the knowledge to prevent it.

I was lucky to be raised in a family that believed in the power of saving and budgeting, and taught me all of their skills, tips, and tricks. And now I want to share those lucky teachings with you — because they are life-changing, and they work. They work when you are starting out with no money, no assets, zip, zero, zilch. And they work later, when you pull yourself out of that situation to a life of more abundance.

This book is based on those lessons, and my success in implementing those strategies in my own life. I've been successfully using these strategies for over 20 years now, and I can tell you, they work.

My hope is that if you're in a world of financial hurt right now, the strategies I share in this book will help you get out of it, and start living the life you want. Just remember that it will take time, practice, and hard work — but all of it will be well worth it in the end!

He who would learn to fly one day must first learn to stand and walk and run and climb and dance; one cannot fly into flying. Friedrich Nietzsche

Who Should Read This Book

This book is for you if :

- You are living paycheck to paycheck and struggling to pay

your bills (but you know that so, onwards…).

- You'd like to use a budgeting system that's easy to use and actually works.
- You want to be in control of your money, rather than have your money control you.
- You feel like your money isn't stretching as far as it should.
- You have one hour per month (15 minutes per week) to put towards maintaining the budgeting system that you'll learn in this book.
- You're having trouble reaching your financial goals.

This Book is NOT For You If

This book is definitely not for you if you want to be taught all about how to invest your money. That is a totally separate topic, and deserves a book of its own!

My view is that before you can even think about investing your money, you need to stop living paycheck to paycheck — and this book will help you do that. Once you've mastered the art of managing your money via a budget that runs like a well-oiled machine, then, and only then, should you start to learn about investing your money. I'll recommend some reading for that at the end of this book!

This book is not for you if you want a magic elixir that will fix everything for you overnight.

This book is not for you if you want advice from someone who is currently broke and living paycheck to paycheck. Wouldn't you rather take your budgeting advice from someone who has figured out how to make their money work for them, and can teach you exactly how they did it so you can do the same? I use these money management strategies every day and they work very well. Let me show you how to do it!

Last, but not least, remember this: For the strategies in this book to be maximally effective, you need to be committed to learning the techniques that this book will teach you, and you need to be willing to stick with it over the long haul.

Never Give Up

Now, I know that you might be one of those people who are in a really tough situation that it seems only a fairy godmother could fix. But if you look deep inside yourself, can you say with 100% certainty that you are doing absolutely everything (and I mean everything!) within your power to maximize the benefits that whatever money you have can provide you with? Is there a chance that your frustration with your financial situation might have caused you to give up on yourself? Is it possible that your financial situation has caused you to lose hope that it can ever get better and you've stopped trying to improve it?

If any of that sounds like you, then I ask you to give yourself another chance at a life that's free from stressing about money.

You're stronger and more capable than you think.

You deserve another chance. Give it to yourself. Never give up.

The strategies that you'll learn in this book can go a long way towards ensuring you get to live a life that's free from most of the stresses about money.

What You Will Learn in This Book

By reading this book, you're going to learn the easy way to put together a budget that will:

- help you pay down bad debt, and avoid getting more
- help you reach your financial goals with greater ease
- provide for your daily monetary needs, both now, and in the

future
- lower or eliminate your worries about money
- take an hour per month or less to keep tabs on
- actually work

You will also learn:

- the 6 most important things you can do to take control of your money
- the 5 biggest benefits to having a budget
- the common misconceptions about budgets
- 10 tips on how to get the right mindset for success
- 11 budget traps, and how to avoid them
- the easiest ways to have more money without earning more
- how to trim your expenses with (almost) no effort
- how to use my free tool, the Money Tracker, to make your own custom system for taking control of your money
- tips that will help you eliminate your debts

My Promise to You

I promise you that if you read this book, and stick with the strategies you'll learn from it, you will dramatically increase your odds of having a more secure financial future and a lot less stress about money in your life.

Don't be the kind of person who procrastinates and makes a bad situation worse.

Be the kind of person who isn't afraid to to tackle a problem head on.

Be the kind of person whom others admire for their tenacity and determination to overcome any roadblocks in their path, and push through to success.

Be the kind of person who takes action now.

The strategies you will learn in this book can create positive, long-lasting results. All you need to do right now to reap those rewards is keep reading.

You can stop living paycheck to paycheck and start to take control of your money right now, today. After that, sit back and enjoy the new life you are creating for yourself, a life where you feel secure and more confident in your ability to manage your money. It's your time.

What is a Budget?

A budget is something that isn't a big deal to implement (once you know how to do it), but can have a HUGE impact on your life.

A budget is nothing more than a way to keep track of how much money you have coming in and how much is being spent, combined with setting financial goals. You choose the goals based on your individual needs and what you want to accomplish. These goals aren't set in stone — they are fluid and will change along with your circumstances.

How Long Will This Take?

The good news is that once you put in the time to set up your budget, it won't take you more than an hour a month to keep tabs on things. I recommend you split this time into about 15 minutes, four times per month (about once a week) since that makes any work you have to do in order to keep this up pretty easy and painless.

But, do be prepared to spend a few hours over this first month to go through the exercises in this book — you need to put in the time to learn these new skills, right? Nothing worth having comes without effort after all!

How to Use This Book

Read it cover to cover! I know… that's such an obvious answer. But some sections in this book are written with the assumption that you already know about the stuff covered in earlier sections, so things will work out better for you if you just read everything in the order that it's presented.

And I know you're probably tempted to skip ahead to making your actual budget, but please hold off on that until you've read through all of the chapters leading up to it! The actual budgeting exercises all depend on you having read and internalized the information presented in the preceding chapters.

You see, before you get into the nitty gritty details of hammering out a budget, custom-made for your unique needs and situation, I want to arm you with all of the information you'll need to maximize your chances of success.

The thing is, we all know the common sense basics behind budgeting, right? But sometimes we just need an extra push to make us follow through and do what needs to be done, right? This book will provide you with that push by reminding you of all the things you may have forgotten about, exposing the budgeting myths that may be preventing you from successfully managing your money, and giving you a hand up via easy tips for maximizing what you've already got!

One of the key tools that will make your budgeting process easier is the free Money Tracker that is included with the purchase of this book. If you haven't done so already, get your Money Tracker at the following link — it will make the rest of the book much easier to follow.

http://averybreyer.com/1hr-budget-how-to-stop-living-paycheck-to-paycheck-opt-in/

That's it!

The 6 Most Important Things You Can Do to Take Control of Your Money

Control your own destiny or someone else will. Jack
Welch

If you do nothing other than these six things, you'll be far more in control of your money, plus worry less about money and your future, compared to most people. Want in? Then keep reading.

1. Track Your Spending

Ok, so this doesn't exactly sounds like buckets of fun. I know. But just think, there's a reason why every successful business tracks their expenses. They don't have a hope in hell of controlling them, if they have no idea what they are in the first place, right? Treat your own finances in a similar fashion and you'll be well on your way to having your own personal finances function as a well-run, profitable business.

Knowledge is power my friend — arm yourself with as much

knowledge about where your money is going as you possibly can!

2. Track Your Income

Well, this one is certainly more fun than step one, and equally important! Tracking your income will give you a baseline maximum level for your expenses. Knowing this number will go a long way to helping you to stay out of bad debt, and making yourself a future that is as worry-free as possible, as far as your finances are concerned.

3. Always Have a Back Up Plan

Things don't always go according to plan, right? So to add an extra layer of protection to your financial well-being, give some thought to how you could earn more money if it ever became necessary. Could you work a second job? Do more overtime at your current job? Start a side business?

Money won't create success, the freedom to make it will. Nelson Mandela

And don't forget to figure out a few ways to cut your expenses if it ever becomes necessary. Think about some of the big ticket items: housing, transportation, and utility bills. If push came to shove, and you HAD to, is there a way for you to make those things significantly less expensive? And then think of some of the stuff you spend money on that you could do without if need be. I'm not saying you have to implement those kinds of changes now, but you should definitely give it some thought so that if there were ever a crisis and you needed to, you'd have a way to slash those costs and ride out the bad times.

4. Get Real about Needs versus Wants

This is related to the back up plan we just talked about. If you ever needed to reduce your spending, the easiest, least painful way of doing it is to cut back on discretionary spending.

He who buys what he does not need steals from himself. Swedish Proverb

Needs should include things like basic shelter, heat, clean water, basic clothing/shoes, and food.

Wants include all the extras. You know, things like:

- Your unlimited text, talk, and data cell phone plan
- Cable TV
- Super-duper-ultra-deluxe-fastest-in-the-country internet plan
- New clothes, just because you were tired of the old ones
- The six pairs of extra shoes you have, just because they make your outfits look "just right"
- Booze (wine, beer, spirits, etc.)

I know my version of wants versus needs is on the strict side, but let's be real — you'll survive without all the wants, right? But...

I'm also not suggesting that you should not spend your money on items from the "wants" list.

There's nothing wrong with using your money to buy those things if you can afford it. But, as you'll see later in this book, being very honest with yourself about which things are truly needed, and which things are optional to spend your money on ("wants") is crucial to being able to budget more effectively and take full control over your money.

5. Relationships and Money: Talk About It!

Money is seen as a taboo topic by a lot of people. But if you're in a serious relationship with someone, it shouldn't be. There are tons of people out there who end up miserable over money, and their relationships are often the cause of it. Avoid that brand of heartache by tackling the issues head on from the start.

If you're in a long-term relationship and pooling your finances via joint bank accounts, taking on shared debts (e.g., co-signing on a mortgage loan together), or signing a lease for an apartment together, I recommend that both of you get on the same page about money asap. What you do affects your partner, and vice versa. Heck, even if you're not pooling your money together right now, if your partner is deep in debt, it'll affect you too, eventually.

Here are a few things you should discuss with one another:

- **Current financial situation:** Both you and your partner should be open with one another about your incomes, expenses, assets, and any debts that either of you have.
- **Financial goals:** You and your partner need to discuss what you want to accomplish with your money. Is saving for retirement a priority right now? Saving for a new car? Saving money for travel? Figure it out.
- **Shared life goals:** There are some goals, like the wish to buy a house someday, or starting a family, that will bring on expenses that will effect both of you. If you spend some time thinking about this ahead of time, the two of you will be in a better position to plan for them.
- **Attitudes about money:** Do you guys tend to believe money is there to be spent right away? Or do you believe saving for the future is really important? Do you feel guilty if you accumulate too much money? How much of your income do you believe you should donate to worthy causes?
- **Separate or Joint Accounts:** Do you believe in combining each of your incomes and expenses into one big pot? Or do you believe each of you should keep your income, bank accounts, and expenses separate, only pooling your funds when necessary for expenses that benefit you both (e.g., housing cost, utility bills etc)
- **Controlling the Money:** Who will be the one to keep track of

expenses? Who will be the one to pay bills? Who will be in charge of keeping an eye on your budget? Or will you share these responsibilities?

Many people avoid discussing these topics because it seems awkward, or they've been taught since childhood that it's rude to discuss money. I'm giving you permission to throw caution to the wind here and discuss away.

If you get involved in a serious relationship with someone, it is of the utmost importance that you get on the same page financially. It is very difficult to take control of your money if your partner's goals are pulling you in the wrong direction. Whereas if you discuss these things, it'll go a long way towards allowing both of you to reach your monetary goals — and as a bonus, that will contribute to a happier, healthier, relationship.

6. Have an Emergency Fund

Now I know that right now you're living paycheck to paycheck, and figuring out how to save up an emergency fund seems impossible. But I'd be letting you down if I didn't at least plant the idea of it into your mind — because once you implement the strategies you'll learn in this book and stop living paycheck to paycheck, you'll have the breathing room you need to figure out how to amass an emergency stash of cash. Sound good?

As you know, there is no quicker way to skewer a budget than to have an expensive emergency crop up that puts you into a huge pile of unwanted debt. Imagine the peace of mind you'd enjoy if you had an emergency fund that you'd saved up ahead of time.

How much less stress would you have in your life if you knew without a doubt that if you lost your job you could survive (and thrive) just fine for six months or more, coasting on your savings?

Experts often recommend establishing an emergency fund that could sustain all of your financial needs for a minimum of six months. And remember, if this seems impossible, please don't worry. It's okay if you don't have this kind of money right now. Just keep in mind that not having the money right now does not mean you won't have the money later on.

Summing Up

You now know some of the most powerful things you can do to take control over your money. All of those things will be accounted for as you go through the process of making your own budget with the Money Tracker later in this book. But first, it would be a good idea to arm you with a motivation booster. The next chapter will do just that, by going through the 5 biggest benefits of having a budget.

The 5 Biggest Benefits of Having a Budget

The budget is not just a collection of numbers, but an expression of our values and aspirations. Jacob Lew

Looking for some extra motivation for making (and sticking with) a budget? Here are the 5 biggest benefits of having a budget.

1. It Improves Your Credit Rating

Because budgeting helps you to keep track of not only how much money is coming in, but how much money is going out, it becomes really easy to plan for expenses. And that means paying your bills on time, and getting the accompanying boost in your credit rating, is easy.

It also makes it a lot easier to avoid credit card debt. If you're not spending more than you earn, you'll never need to carry a balance on your credit card.

And what does that have to do with your credit rating?

Part of your credit score is based on the percentage of available credit that you actually use. So if you carry a significant balance on your credit cards, your credit score can decrease, even if you're making the minimum payments on time.

2. It Lowers Stress

Having a budget means that you always know exactly how much money you're earning each month, and exactly where every penny is going.

Having a budget means you almost completely eliminate the worries that unexpected large expenses bring, since you've already planned for and saved for those things.

Imagine it's getting close to Christmas time. You have a large extended family, and it's expected that you participate in buying gifts for everyone. And then there's the "Secret Santa" gift exchange at work, and a handful of holiday parties where you're expected to bring a bottle of wine. The extra expenses add up. Before you know it, you've spent $1500 more than usual this month.

But it's ok, right? You still have enough money left in your bank account, and if you're careful, you can make it through the end of the month without going into debt.

A few days after Christmas, you're suffering record levels of stress.

Your car just broke down and the bill to fix it is going to be $1600 or more. Then your dog got sick and the vet bill was another $600. Oh #$%@.

You only have $700 left in your bank account, and there's still a week-and-a-half until payday. Payday will bring in about $1500, so you'll still be short on funds to pay both bills on time, unless you go into credit card debt to make up the shortfall. The thought of paying the outrageously high interest rates on your credit card is killing you.

Now do you think that would have happened if you had a budget, and it was easy to see ahead of time that those expenses were coming up? (Yes, even the car breaking down can be budgeted for in advance if you use the systems that you'll be taught in this book.) And even better, what if your budget kept track of things like the need to save up for Christmas expenses throughout the year, so the extra money would have been there for you?

Having a budget that helps you stay on track with your savings needs can completely eliminate these kinds of stresses from your life.

Remember the free download of the Money Tracker that was included with your purchase of this book? It will help you take care of these things in advance, and prevent these kinds of stressful situations from cropping up in the first place.

3. It Keeps You Honest

Keeping a budget, which includes tracking your spending, keeps you honest.

Honest with yourself, that is.

Knowledge is power, and by keeping track of what you're spending, you won't be able to trick yourself into thinking you're managing your money better than you actually are.

It's so easy to take out $20 from the ATM machine, and before you know it, it's spent on who knows what. Was it for a groceries? Was it for buying that coffee and donut every day as a treat to yourself because you're feeling stressed out and really needed the boost? You'll never be able to remember, let alone control it, if you don't track it.

4. It Helps You Achieve Your Goals

Whether your goals are conservative and all you want is to be secure in the knowledge that you'll always have enough money to pay for necessities each month, or you have big lofty goals like saving up for a car, house, or vacation, a budget can get you there with far more ease than simply going with the flow and hoping for the best.

It's much harder to get those things if you don't have a money plan that you can stick to. Leaving your goals to chance only lessens your chance of achieving them. So make a budget, stick to it, and you'll have more of the things that you want.

5. It Helps You Secure Your Basic Needs Now and in the Future

We all have non-negotiables that we need money for: food, shelter, basic clothing, etc. Having a budget ensures that you know exactly how much money to set aside each month for these necessities, and helps you plug any income gaps that could put that in jeopardy.

Summing Up

Learning about the benefits of having a budget, as you have in this chapter, is very important to keeping your motivation and desire to follow through strong. But it's not everything you need to know. In the next chapter, we're going to cover some of the misconceptions about budgeting — this will be one more weapon in your arsenal, to help ensure that you stay strong and stick to your budget and financial goals.

5 Budget Myths Explained

The great enemy of truth is very often not the lie, deliberate, contrived, and dishonest, but the myth, persistent, persuasive, and unrealistic. John F. Kennedy.

There are loads of untrue myths out there about budgeting. I don't want those untruths to stop you from doing the best thing you could ever do for your financial future: making a budget. After reading this chapter, you'll be way too smart to fall for these myths.

Myth #1: They are Too Restrictive

A good budget is nothing more than a tool that helps you reach your financial goals, while keeping track of your earnings, spending, and savings. Keeping track of your money gives you choice. No more will you find yourself helpless after happily spending the money in your savings account, thinking there's nothing else you need it for, only to find yourself stressed out due to not having the money a month later when a bill for a large once-yearly expense arrives.

I would argue that a good budget does not restrict you, but provides you with freedom. It puts you firmly in the drivers seat when it comes to your money. You are the boss — you are the one that decides what to spend your money on, rather than leaving it to chance or mistake. You ensure that you always have enough money to pay for necessities, and, with planning, some fun things too. What could be better than that?

Meet Angie. She's always hated budgets, and thought they weren't necessary. So it won't come as a surprise to you that she simply buys things if she has cash in her bank account, and doesn't worry too much about money otherwise. But then she's always caught off guard during months when unavoidable expenses hit: It's her mother's 60th birthday this month and she wanted to buy her mom something extra special to celebrate this milestone (but whoops, her life is so hectic that she forgot about that when she splurged on take-out for dinner too many times last month when she should have saved the money for her mother's gift instead!!) Now she doesn't have the money to buy her mother the kind of gift she wanted to. She's stressed. If she buys her mother the gift she wants to, the one that her mother so deserves, she'll be behind and have to rack up some credit card debt to cover it.

Meet Tim. He is a smart guy who keeps tabs on how much money he makes and how much he spends, and he always puts money aside for future expenses. He always has enough money to pay his bills, and always has enough set aside in savings to allow him to take advantage of opportunities that are important to him and happen to cost money. Jealous? Don't be. Just become another Tim. It might take more time than you'd like to get there, but all of your efforts and hard work will be worth it, I promise.

Remember: Running out of money is restrictive. Budgeting to ensure you always have enough money to meet your needs is freedom.

Myth #2: A Budget Will Prevent Me From Buying the Things I Want

Nope. A good budget will do the precisely the opposite. A good budget will make it more likely that you can buy the things you want over the long term.

You might be tempted to say, "Forget budgeting — I'll just buy whatever I want now, and worry about the future later." And then the future comes, you're broke, neck-deep in credit card debt, and your hands are tied — you can barely manage to squeak out enough money for food and rent... never mind spending money on fun stuff.

Meanwhile, if you'd simply made a budget that fit your priorities and goals, and stuck to it, odds are you'd have spent your entire life being able to easily afford the things you need, and lots of fun things that fell into the "want" category.

Which situation would you rather be in? Obviously there are no guarantees, but making a budget and sticking to it will dramatically increase your odds of living a financially comfortable life.

Myth #3: I Make Plenty of Money, So I Don't Need a Budget

I know, you're probably wondering what this myth is doing here in a book for people who are living paycheck to paycheck. But the thing is, I'm optimistic for you — I don't believe you will always be living paycheck to paycheck. I believe that you can change your situation and so should you!

So here's the thing. When the day comes that you have more than enough money to cover your expenses, don't slip up and stop maintaining your budget.

Don't be like David. He's a successful businessman who makes $80,000 a year, lives in a nice house in an average middle class neighbourhood, drives a $40,000 minivan, and goes on vacation once a year to all-inclusive resorts in the Caribbean. Before you

say he's doing awesome, let's peek behind the curtain…

After income taxes, his effective take-home pay is only about $60,000 per year. He spends $10,000 per year on vacations, leaving him $50,000 per year leftover ($4166 per month).

His mortgage balance is $300,000. The monthly payments on that, even with a super low interest rate of only 3.44%, is $1333/month, assuming it'll take him 30 years to pay off. So now he has only $2833/month leftover.

His property taxes for that nice house are about $4000 per year (averages out to $333/month). So that means he actually has only $2500/month left over.

Oh, wait… he still owes some money on that minivan he just bought, so we can't forget to add in his monthly car payments of $771.

His son plays sports at a high level, and he cost of lessons, uniforms, and other equipment average $400 per month.

His daughter's extra-curricular activities set them back another $300 per month.

So now he has only $1029 per month left over.

He is still making payment on his student loans from college, which amounts to $500 per month.

So he really only has $529/month leftover to cover feeding his family, his utility bills, saving for retirement and other household expenses. By the time he pays for those things every month, he's dipping into his line of credit, and accumulating credit card debt.

Whoops. Life doesn't look so good after all, does it?

Sure, most people won't be quite as irresponsible with their money as

David (hello, fancy vacations when he can't afford it!), but as you can see, having lots of money does not mean you can throw caution to the wind and skip budgeting. It's too easy for things to get out of control.

Budgeting will help you get further with the money you have, so you don't have to work as hard, or as long.

Myth #4: Budgeting Takes a Lot of Time

Wrong. Once you have it set up, you'll spend no more than 15 minutes a week to keep it going. You'll learn how to do that by the end of this book.

Myth #5: I Spend Less Than I Earn, So I Don't Need a Budget

Again, I know you're living paycheck to paycheck, so maybe the possibility that you could be spending less than you earn seems far off. But believe me, it's probably a lot closer than you think. And when you get there, I don't want you to fall off track. Having a well-designed budget, the kind you'll learn how to make in this book, helps to ensure that you'll keep firmly on track towards your goals.

Let's say you want to save up for an emergency fund, a down-payment on a house, or for a once-in-a-lifetime vacation. Keeping a budget will ensure you put aside enough money each month to reach that goal, and will prevent you from accidentally spending too much of your hard-earned money on other discretionary things.

I'd like to live as a poor man with lots of money.
Pablo Picasso

Summing Up

Now that you've learned the truth about some of the budgeting myths out there, it's time to learn how how to get into the right mindset for successful budgeting. This often-overlooked component of budgeting is critical in helping you to avoid talking yourself out of success and giving up too soon, among other things.

10 Tips: How to Get The Right Mindset for Success

No person is free who is not master of himself. Epictetus

If you don't have the right mindset, you are destined to fail when it comes to sticking to your budget. Here are 10 tips for getting your mind in the right place and avoiding common budgeting traps.

1. Avoid shiny object syndrome by pre-planning which shiny objects actually matter to you. Shiny object syndrome is when you are easily tempted by the latest and greatest things that money can buy. And it's deadly for anyone who wants to take control of their money. Maybe you want to pay off your credit card debt or student loans, save up for an emergency fund or a new house or a vacation. Whatever it is, keep that goal firmly in mind whenever you are tempted by some other "shiny object." When you have a clear picture in your mind of what you really want to get with your money, it'll become ridiculously easy to deny yourself other temptations that come your way.

2. Adopt a systems mindset. You must embrace the idea of using a system to get you to your financial goals. Without a proper system in place, it's all too easy to drift along aimlessly and go off track.

Creating a budget with the Money Tracker is the method I recommend, but feel free to use another if that suits you better. The point is, pick a system that works for you and stick with it!

3. Promise yourself that you will make at least one small step towards your goal each and every day, and savour these small wins towards reaching your goal. This can be as simple as bringing a bagged lunch to work, so you can save the money you would have spent eating out for something more important to you.

4. "Do. Or do not. There is no try." (Yoda) Ok, so I'm geeking out a bit here, quoting an alien from a Star Wars movie. But you know what, Yoda had it right. If controlling your money is important to you, just do it. Don't say you'll "try." Sure there are some times in life where it's ok to just try. But when it comes to making a budget, and prioritizing your spending, there is no such as thing as try. You can either do it, or not do it. I bet you know in your heart of hearts that you need to do this. So jump in with both feet and commit to it.

5. Decide to stick with this for a minimum of 12 months. Here's the thing — any new habit is harder at first, but the longer you keep it in your life, the easier it becomes to continue on with it. So decide right now that you will do this for a 12 month minimum. Not only will keeping up your budget be easier the longer you do it, but the benefits you reap financially will become much more obvious the longer you're at this, and that will help you to retain the motivation to continue on this path to success. So give it a good chance — you'd hate to quit just when you were on the cusp of success, right?

6. Learn from your failures. Don't push failures out of your mind until you've given yourself a chance to reflect on them first. You can't learn from them if you pretend they never happened, right? So whenever something goes wrong with your budgeting, take the time to think it over and figure out how you might keep this from happening again. Learn from it, and grow stronger! The failure wasn't for nothing if it makes you stronger and wiser in the future. Once you've taken whatever lessons you can from your failures, move on. Because there is no sense beating yourself up over things that can't be undone.

7. Plan for worst-case scenarios. No one likes to think about the worst case scenario for their financial life. But to maximize your odds of success, you should. Think about various worst-case scenarios and figure out how you can minimize the impact it would have on you. For example, you could set a goal to save up enough money in your emergency fund to sustain you for six months in case you ever lose your job. Or maybe your mortgage is a variable rate — what if interest rates double by the time your mortgage is up for renewal? What would that do to your mortgage payments? What can you do now, to make it easier on you if that disastrous situation came to pass? For example, simply saving up a sizable emergency fund will go a long way to helping you ride out many of those worst-case scenarios.

8. Adopt an optimistic mindset about your ability to control your finances. Ironic that I mention that right after asking you to consider the worst-case scenarios, I know. But hear me out. You need to believe that things can work out for you, that you can control the outcome, even if calamities happen. It is very hard to ride out a worst-case scenario if you are pessimistic and feel powerless to come out the other side intact. On the other hand, if you feel deep down that you can handle   whatever comes your way, if you feel that you can do something about it that will make it better eventually, it will help you stick to your plan and not give up.

Believe you can and you're halfway there. Theodore Roosevelt

9. Focus on the results you want to achieve when making decisions about money. Any time you're tempted to stray from your budget, ask yourself first if this will help you to achieve the goals you've set for yourself.

10. Adopt a growth mindset. "This growth mindset is based on the belief that your basic qualities are things you can cultivate through your efforts. Although people may differ in every which way — in

their initial talents and aptitudes, interests, or temperaments —
everyone can change and grow through application and
experience." (Carol Dweck, Stanford University[1]) So if you've
always thought of yourself as being lousy with your money, this
doesn't mean you're destined to always be that way.

*Do the one thing you think you cannot do. Fail at it.
Try again. Do better the second time. The only
people who never tumble are those who never mount
the high wire. This is your moment. Own it.* Oprah
Winfrey

I love this quote because it acknowledges the fact that yes, you can
fail, and so what, just try again! Too often, we put pressure on
ourselves to avoid failure at all costs — but that can be paralyzing if
the fear of failure causes us to not try at all.

Adopt a growth mindset and choose to improve your skills; do not fear
failure — with time and practice, you can become excellent at
managing your money. Who you have been up until now does not
mean you cannot become different going forward.

Summing Up

Now you know how important it is to adopt the right mindset if you
want to succeed at budgeting. You've come a long way, and learned so
much in the last few chapters. But you're not done yet. Now it's time
to arm yourself with knowledge about why people fail to stick to a
budget, and how to prevent that. Are you ready? Then turn the page!

11 Budget Traps (And How to Avoid Them)

I have not failed. I've just found 10,000 ways that won't work. Thomas A. Edison

Ok, so there are tons of budget traps that can cause you to fail to stick to a budget, but here are some of the most common ones:

1. You totally cut out the fun. Don't do that. Even if your budget is ridiculously tight, there is almost always some little treat you can afford. Even if it's as small as a chocolate bar once a week. And if your budget has more wiggle room, then by all means put some money aside each month for more pricy fun such as vacations to somewhere exotic.

2. You forgot to include expenses that only come up once in a while. Many people set up a budget and only take into account regular monthly expenses like food, utilities, rent/mortgage payments and entertainment. But you also need to put aside money each month for "unexpected" expenses, such as car or home maintenance, once yearly bills for insurance, taxes (e.g., property tax or income tax), Christmas shopping, and even retirement savings!

3. You feel like there's no point since you never have enough money to cover your expenses anyways. Don't forget that it is a very rare person indeed who honestly can't do something to improve a situation like that. If you stick with me, and follow the advice in this book, odds are good you'll see that you have a greater ability to control this issue than you think. So don't give up on your finances just yet — it's too early for that!

4. You're using the wrong tools. You have to choose a tool for tracking your earnings and expenses that is easy for you to use, and easy to understand. If whatever tool you're currently using isn't working for you, then by all means, switch to something else. I've always used the Money Tracker, which is included as a free download with this book. However, there are alternatives that many people find helpful also.

5. You made a budget and treated it as if it's set in stone forever. That's the wrong way to go about it — life is unpredictable sometimes, and circumstances change — your budget needs to be adjusted when this happens. If you follow the advice in this book, you'll see that revisiting your budget happens automatically each month, so you'll know when you need to make adjustments.

6. You spend more than you earn and don't know when to say "no" when it comes to spending your money. No worries, you're not the first, and you certainly won't be the last person to have this problem. But the good news is that if you track your earnings and expenses, it becomes easy, common sense even, to figure out when you ought to say "yes" or "no" to a new purchase. The Money Tracker will also help you to know, at a glance, how much "extra" money you have available to spend on things that aren't in your budget. Lastly, figuring out concrete goals for your money will also help you resist the temptation to spend unnecessarily — when you have something better in mind that you want that money to go towards, it's easy to say "no" to the latest temptation if it doesn't fit your long-term goals.

7. You're too busy — it takes too much time to keep track of your money. Using a system like the one I teach you in this book will allow you to minimize the time needed to track your money. Honestly, the most time-consuming part is setting up a spreadsheet to track everything, and I've already done that for you (you guessed it, it's the free Money Tracker). All that's left is for you to spend 15 minutes a week, at most, jotting down your earnings and spending. That's an average of less than three minutes a day if you spread it out over the week!

8. Your friendships are expensive. A lot of people have this problem, and you're not alone. Do you have friends who like to do things that cost a lot of money whenever you see each other? You know, stuff like going out for dinner at pricey places, or spending a lot of money on going to the latest movie. Ladies, maybe your friends love regular girl's shopping weekends where everyone shops and spends with wild abandon, all while staying at costly hotel. Gentlemen, maybe your friends like to blow wads of cash on beer, paintball, or laser tag. The only fix is to give yourself permission to stop trying to keep up with them. If they all order an expensive dinner, eat at home beforehand and order a coffee at the restaurant instead of a pricey meal. Sure, it'll feel weird at first, but you'll get over it… trust me! Instead of going out to a movie, try suggesting popcorn and movie night at your place instead. And don't feel bad about skipping expensive outings if there is no way to make it fit your budget.

9. You're trying to keep up with the Joneses. If all of your neighbours drive a nice looking car, it's hard to be the only one who drives a rust bucket. If most people in your social circle have a huge house, it's hard to say no to that and buy a small fixer-upper. If everyone around you seems to have nice furniture and the latest video game system for their kids, it can be hard to be the only one with a torn sofa and the hand-me-down game system that was a hit 10 years ago. If everyone you hang out with has spendy habits whenever you go out (see #8 above), it's hard to be the only one trying to spend less. But keep in mind that all of these people you are trying to keep up with may be deep in debt. These people may very well be having a hell of a time paying their bills on time, if they manage it at all. So take the pressure off yourself and just be you, thrifty habits and all. You'll feel less stress overall, and anyone who is worth caring about will understand.

Too many people spend money they earned..to buy things they don't want..to impress people that they don't like. Will Rogers

10. You don't know where to start. Hey, don't worry about this. Most people aren't born with a natural talent for managing their money. Most people need to be taught this skill, so don't be too hard on yourself. All you need to do is make a commitment to learn, and be patient enough to see it through. You'll learn everything you need to get started in this book, and those skills will last you a lifetime.

11. You worry about what people will think of you. Especially if others in your social circles tend to spend a lot more than you can afford, you may worry that if you don't do the same, they will think you are a cheapskate. But keep in mind that as I mentioned in point #9, for all you know, they may be deep in debt due to their freewheeling, spending ways. And if they are not in debt, but just make a ton of money and can afford it, then no one in their right mind should expect you to do likewise if you are not in the same financial situation. And even if you can afford it, if you don't wish to spend your money on those things, you shouldn't. It's your money, and your life — your spending should align with *your* goals — not those of someone else. I humbly suggest that you decide from here on out, that what other people think of you is none of your business. It's easier said than done, I know. But trust me, with practice it gets easier.

Summing Up

By reading this chapter, you are now wiser than most people when it comes to budget traps. But I want to arm you with even more information to make it as easy as possible to live within your means. This next chapter will do just that. You're about to learn some of the easiest ways to have more money, without earning more!

The Easiest Way to Have More Money, Without Earning More

Never spend your money before you have it. Thomas Jefferson

The easiest, most effective way to get more money, without needing to earn more, is to avoid taking on any bad debt, and if you already have it, pay it off as soon as humanly possible.

Bad Debt — Common Sources and How To Avoid Them

This next bit will help to shore up your resistance to the temptation to take on this kind of debt, and if you already have bad debt, it will help you resist the temptation to take on any more in future.

For the purposes of our little chat here, bad debt includes any debt that isn't making you more money than the interest you're paying on it.

Bad debt can suck the life out of you. It is relentless. And it kills your ability to save.

We are constantly bombarded with advertising and salespeople trying to make us think that getting a loan to pay for things we don't need is normal. Just today as I wrote this, I see on the Canadian Imperial Bank of Commerce (CIBC) website that they are suggesting their personal loan products if you want to take a vacation, among other things.

Clearly CIBC is more concerned with making money on the interest you'll pay than whether or not a loan for these purposes is really a good idea for you.

Let's go through some of the common sources of bad debt, and the reasons why you ought to avoid them (to shore up your resistance to the temptation to use borrowed money for these things in future!) The end result: more money in your pocket.

Car Loans

If you have a car loan, pay it off as soon as humanly possible. All that interest you're paying is eating into your income, and I'm sure you'd much rather spend the money on things more useful than interest on a car loan.

Sure, you can afford the monthly payments, but imagine how much extra you are paying for that car once you add up all the interest payments?

For example, let's say you treat yourself to a brand new car for $30,000. You get a nice low interest rate of only 5%, and you agree to pay it off within 60 months, or five years.

Not bad, huh?

But wait.

You're going to pay $3968 in interest over those five years.

That money could have gone towards other expenses that you desperately need the money for. It could have eased the tightness in your budget for food, clothing, and shelter.

Aren't there a million other things you can think of where that $3958 would have been better spent?

So I'd like to suggest that you be patient, and save up the $30,000 cash before you buy that car.

Or better still, buy a used car for a lot less. What if you researched the used car market and bought a reliable, low maintenance used vehicle instead? I bet you could find a good one for $10,000 or less.

Then you'd have not only the $3968 in interest payments to spend on other, much better stuff, but also $20,000 extra! That's huge!

Say it with me: "$23,958 extra to spend on whatever I please."

P.S. Not sure where to start with research on reliable used cars? If you're Canadian, check out Phil Edmonston's Lemon-Aid Guides. I buy the most current issue of his used car buying guide whenever I'm in the market for a used car, and his advice has never let me down. Quite frankly, even if you live in the U.S., I suspect much of his advice would work for you too, since many models of cars are available in both countries. Or make a quick trip to your local library or bookstore and you'll see lots of options for good info on recommended makes and models of used cars.

Ready to get even MORE extreme?

Ok, it's time to get really crazy now. Consider, seriously, whether or not you could manage without a car.

I know… if you're someone who has always had their own car, that sounds insane, right? But think about it for a minute.

Because it's not just the cash required up front to buy the car. It's the maintenance, repairs, gas, and insurance that eat up a lot of money too. Add these numbers up, and then decide if the price of car ownership is really worth it for you.

If you're fortunate enough to live in a place with a good public transit system in place, you'll save thousands of dollars compared to owning your own car.

Now I'm certainly not saying you shouldn't have a car — only you know the answer to that. All I'm saying is don't assume owning your own car is the only choice you have because that's what you've always done — give some thought to how your finances and day-to-day life would look if you didn't own a car, and instead, relied on public transit, plus the occasional ride from friends, family, or a taxi.

Furniture Loans

Please tell me you wouldn't ever get a loan to pay for furniture. Surely you don't want to suffer from the drain on your bank account when the interest payments kick in. The alternative is to make do with what you have — because no one ever suffered much from not having a new sofa.

Read this and be forever immunized against the temptation of getting a costly loan for furniture.

Furniture salespeople try to tempt you by saying you get your shiny new furniture to take home and enjoy right now, and owe nothing for a year. "Just pay it all off before the year is done," the sales person says, "and it won't cost you any extra. This gives you time to save up the money, while enjoying the furniture right now!"

The reality is…

Every time you try to enjoy your new debt-ridden piece of furniture, you have this thing hanging over your head… this threat that if you don't pay up within a year, they'll saddle you with payments and a likely outrageous rate of interest tacked on. How does that feel?

Sure, based on how things are right now, you think you'll probably have the money to pay for it in a year. But what if you won't? What if something unexpected happens and it eats up that money you thought you'd have to pay for the furniture? Why take that chance when you can get by on your old furniture?

Wouldn't you enjoy that new furniture much more if you knew you'd already paid for it in full? That it was 100% yours with no strings attached?

My German Shepherd dog clawed my couch once. Badly. The newly torn upholstery turned my beloved couch into a bit of an embarrassment, really. So I covered it with a somewhat decorative blanket every time I had company over. And I put a matching cushion against the arm rest to cover the stuffing that poked through there. I made do with my clawed up, torn couch. For about seven years.

Maybe that sounds pathetic to you. But in my mind, I felt like I didn't need to prove myself to anyone, and if they had a problem with my couch, they could just choose not to look at it. It was simply not my problem.

So make do with what you already have, and don't you dare buy a new piece of furniture unless you a) don't have anything more important to spend your money on, and b) you have the cash to pay for it up front. Ok?

And making do with what you have isn't only for the broke.

Do you know what? Even if you have the cash for a new couch it doesn't mean you need to use it for that.

At the time I lived with that torn couch, I literally had enough cash in the bank to buy a whole bunch of new couches.

So why the heck didn't I?

For starters, I still owned that dog. Why waste money on a new couch that he'd probably just tear again, right?

Also, more importantly, I was saving up to buy rental properties that would fund my future retirement. And blowing money on a new couch would do zip to help accomplish that. Finally, since it wasn't a necessity either, it didn't make the cut for things that I was willing to spend my hard-earned money on. Every bit of savings counted!

Unless you're rich, you need to prioritize your spending.

What if I'm desperate, I have nothing, and need to furnish my place? Then can I take the no payments for one year deal? I'm sure I'll have the money by then.

Nope! You have other, better choices. Ask family and friends if anyone is getting rid of unneeded furniture. Start checking out garage sales and thrift stores. Buy the minimum you need to get by, save up more money, and then buy the stuff you really want once you can properly afford it (i.e., you have the cash.) So what if your furniture isn't the most amazing right now? You'll have way less stress in your life if you buy things as you can afford them, rather than gambling that you'll have the money later when the loan comes due.

You can live with far fewer things than you think you can. Society puts all of these expectations on us to have magazine-worthy homes, new furniture, pricey manicures, a closet full of clothes (half of which we probably never wear), a new car, and on it goes. But all of these expectations are bogus. They are designed to encourage you to part with your money and make the companies that sell these things rich. Don't buy into it unless you can honestly afford it.

Vacation Loans

This is never, ever something you should do. In fact, vacation loans are even worse than furniture loans because no one will ever tell you there are no payments for a year. Instead, you'll owe interest from the day the bank gives you the money.

It is not normal to use a loan to take a vacation. And don't let a bank convince you otherwise.

You'll never enjoy things to the max if you have debt hanging over your head because of it — it's far better to buy things free and clear as much as possible. And besides, I'm sure I don't need to remind you that the interest you'd pay on a vacation loan will only mean you paid far more for that holiday than you should have, and now have even less money left for other things in future.

Credit Card Debt

Credit cards can be a great way to pay for things, and very convenient. But if you don't pay them off in full each month, you end up saddled with outrageous amounts of interest.

The secret to avoiding credit card debt for most people is to figure out how much they'll pay in interest if they go that route. Odds are, if you calculate these figures, you'll be so disgusted at the amount of money wasted that you'll never succumb to the temptation of going into credit card debt again. Always remember that the credit card companies are in the business of making money, and they make a ton of money off people who don't pay off their balances each month.

For example, let's say you consider making a $3000 purchase that you would fund via credit card debt, and making only the minimum payments each month. Let's say your credit card charges 19% interest (sometimes called APR, or annual percentage rate), and the minimum percentage of the balance that must be paid off is 2% (these figures will vary from card to card, so check with your credit card company to see what rates apply to any credit cards you have.) We will also assume, for the purposes of this example, that you make only the minimum monthly payments, while never adding any additional charges to this credit card. Your minimum monthly payment would be around $60 to start with.

Some people might say that doesn't sound so bad.

But hold on.

How much interest will you pay over the lifetime of the debt? In the 22.1 years that it will take to pay off, you'll pay over $7000 in interest. So your $3000 purchase costs you over $10,000 in the end.

And will this purchase even last you the entire 22.1 years it takes to pay off? You know they don't tend to make things as well as they used to, so it'll likely be a miracle if your purchase lasts 22.1 years. Odds are you'd have to buy a replacement while still paying off the debt for the first one. Not so great, right?

Here is a link to a handy credit card payment calculator:

http://www.creditcards.com/calculators/minimum-payment.php

You can enter in the amount of the debt, the percentage of the balance that has to be paid off each month, and your interest rate. The calculator takes care of the rest, letting you know how long you'd take to pay it off, and how much interest you'd be paying in the meantime. It's a great reality check, and is sure to help you resist the temptation to accumulate any credit card debt.

Summing Up

Do you see now how easy it is to stretch your money further if you resist the temptation to make the banks and credit card companies rich by buying things on credit? If you commit from this day forward to make do with what you have, and only buy the kinds of things discussed in this chapter if you have the cash to pay for them, you'll soon be reaping the financial rewards!

In the next chapter, you're going to learn some powerful strategies for saving money on everyday expenses — which is yet another way to put free money in your pocket!

How to Trim Your Expenses With (Almost) No Effort

Though small was your allowance
You saved a little store
And those who save a little
Shall get a plenty more.
William Makepeace Thackeray

When you're living paycheck to paycheck, it's important that you do everything you can to trim your expenses. But you might as well start with things that are easy to do and take almost no effort, right?

Have you heard of the 80-20 rule? In case you haven't, it basically means that 20% of your efforts result in 80% of the results. So, since we all have busy lives, it makes sense to concentrate your efforts on the 20% for maximal results with a minimum of effort.

Here are some strategies from that 20% for trimming your expenses — including ways to save on food, clothing, health, home and cleaning, accommodations, children, and banking.

Food — 4 Ways to Trim Your Costs

1. Shop at a grocery store that automatically matches the prices in their competitors' flyers. I loved doing this because I didn't have to search their competitors' flyers to get the best deal — my favourite grocery store would do it for me, and the prices would automatically scan at the lower price when checking out. So look around your local neighbourhood and see if there is a store that does this — not only will it save you time, but money too. With almost no effort.

2. Stock up when costly items that store well go on on sale. So here's the thing — if you try to keep track of what the regular price is for all of your purchases so as to know a good deal when you see it, you'll go crazy. It's simply too much for the average person to keep track of. So use the 80-20 rule and stick to tracking prices of items that'll give you the most bang for your buck: the most costly items that you tend to buy, which also tend to store well over the long term.

Take meat, for example. The almost-no-effort way to save a ton of money on that is to watch the flyers of your favourite grocery store and only buy meat when it is on sale. Once it goes on sale, buy enough of it to last until the next sale comes up, wrap it well, and freeze it until you're ready to use it. Using this method, I was able to consistently buy my meat for almost half price.

However, there are sales, and there are *sales*. I used to shop at one store where one of my favourite cuts of meat would sell at regular price for about $5.99 per pound. I knew that every few weeks it would go on sale for only $2.99 per pound. But while I was waiting for the $2.99 per pound price to come up, I'd see it on sale for anywhere from $3.99 to $4.99 per pound. Since I knew that it would eventually go on sale for $2.99 per pound, I'd always wait for that price — the best price — before I'd part with my money and buy some. You'll see that this kind of thing is really easy to do once you get started.

If you're more ambitious, and have the time, you can apply this strategy to canned goods and any other products that keep well long-term.

3. Buy store brands whenever possible. So I totally get that sometimes the store brand of your favourite food isn't as tasty as the brand name. But lots of times, you'll find the store brand is totally fine — not to mention much less costly than name brand products. And the beauty of this is that store brands are almost always the least costly item in their category, thus eliminating the need for you to waste your mental energy trying to compare prices or clip coupons.

Another option is coupon clipping, but it doesn't fit the almost-no-effort category for most people. It can take ages to collect enough coupons to amount to significant savings, especially since you usually have to slug though multiple flyers, newspapers, and online sites to find them. Also, you need to be careful not to let the coupons tempt you into buying costly items that you usually wouldn't spend money on. So if you have the time, then by all means go for it — but if you don't have time, I wouldn't feel bad about skipping this one.

4. Don't buy pre-prepared food — cook from scratch instead. The cost of eating pre-prepared food adds up. Sure, it's convenient as all heck, but it's way more costly than preparing your own food. The next time you're at the grocery store, compare the cost of buying a ready-to-eat lasagna versus making your own. Compare the price of those ready-to-eat salads versus the cost of making your own from scratch. The price difference is incredible. An easy way to avoid most of the pre-packaged food is to do most of your shopping in the outer perimeter of the store: the fresh produce section, the bakery, the meat department, and the dairy aisle. This way you'll only need to round out your purchases with a minimum of items from the central aisles of the store.

If the idea of cooking from scratch seems like it would take too long, you need to know it doesn't have to. Here are some time-saving tips:

- Use a slow cooker. Just toss all of your ingredients into it in the morning, and eight hours later you have a delicious meal hot and ready to eat. Your supper can literally be cooking while you're at work.

- Cook in bulk. When making things that freeze well like chili and meat sauce, double or triple the recipe, then freeze the leftovers in meal-sized portions. It's almost the same amount of work as it would be to prepare a single batch, but gives you double or triple the meals.
- Make one-pot meals whenever possible. This cuts down on clean up, giving you more time for other things.

Clothing — 8 Ways to Save

1. Don't buy it unless you need it. You'll be amazed at how little you'll spend on clothing if you follow this one rule. Basically, the idea is that you only buy new clothes to replace those that have worn out (assuming you actually need a replacement, of course.) And you don't add any new items to your wardrobe unless it's actually necessary. Ditto for footwear.

2. Consider shopping at secondhand or thrift stores. Need I say more? You know you'll get things for dirt cheap here — this is a great way to go if you really need to cut your clothing expenses down to an absolute minimum.

3. Buy out of season whenever possible. And the next best thing is to buy at the end of the season. These are the times when you'll find things marked down to rock-bottom prices, with discounts of 70% not uncommon. This can save you a ton of money over the long term.

4. Avoid items that need to be dry-cleaned. You'll end up paying for the article of clothing many times over by the time you take into account the cleaning costs. Stick to machine washable clothing.

5. Take good care of your clothes. Follow the care instructions on the labels to get the maximum life out of your clothing. If you can make it last longer, you won't have to spend as much money over your lifetime on replacements.

6. Avoid fad fashions. Stick to items of clothing that are fashionable now, and are likely to remain that way for years to come. That way you won't have to spend money to replace a perfectly good piece of clothing merely because it was last year's look and now you'd "look funny" wearing it.

7. Make small, discreet repairs to clothing rather than toss them out. Have you ever had the zipper break on an otherwise good jacket? Chances are replacing the zipper (easily done by a seamstress) is less expensive than buying a new jacket. Sometimes an otherwise perfectly good shirt will end up with a seam that bursts; with an inexpensive needle and thread, it's super easy to stitch that up yourself, and no one will be the wiser. Or maybe a button has popped off — save it and re-attach it once you're home. Trust me, you don't have to be "good at" sewing to make these kinds of small repairs. And if you've never done it before, a quick search of Google or YouTube will bring up all the instruction you need to be successful.

8. If you'll only wear it once, borrow it. Sometimes things come up where we need a special outfit that'll never be worn again. Ask around and see if anyone you know can lend it to you. If you can't find anyone to borrow from, so be it — you'll have to buy it after all. But it can't hurt to ask.

Health: 18 Ways to Slash Your Healthcare Costs

You can minimize any expenses due to health concerns by preventing them in the first place. Here are four things you should focus on:

1. Get regular exercise. We all know we should get more exercise, but few of us get enough. The Harvard School of Public Health has loads of information on their website explaining exactly what we should be aiming for, whether you're young or old, and I highly recommend you check it out.

www.hsph.harvard.edu/nutritionsource/physical-activity-guidelines/

2. Maintain a healthy weight. I know I keep saying this, but it's true: Knowledge is power! Don't stick your head in the sand over this issue — find out your numbers and take control! Being overweight is proven, without a doubt, to dramatically increase your odds of all kinds of expensive (and unpleasant) maladies, everything from cancer to heart attacks and strokes. Sure, some people will be lucky and avoid these negative outcomes, but most won't, so you owe it to yourself to do everything you can to maintain a healthy weight. There are two major figures you need to know about: your BMI, and your waist circumference. Your BMI should ideally be 24.9 or less, and you can use this handy BMI calculator to find out what yours is:

http://www.nhlbi.nih.gov/health/educational/lose_wt/BMI/bmicalc.htm

For more information on what measurement you should aim for in your waist circumference, head over to this page on the National Heart, Lung, and Blood Institute's website:

http://www.nhlbi.nih.gov/health/educational/lose_wt/risk.htm

If both your BMI and waist circumference are in the ideal range, then you're already doing a lot to preserve your health and save money on health expenses. And if you got bad news when you checked your numbers, then I say you deserve major props for at least finding out where you're at. Now you know what you need to aim for, and that's the first step.

3. Eat a well-balanced diet. Did you know that when you eat, experts recommend half your plate should be filled with an assortment of fruits and vegetables? Most people don't know this, so don't feel bad if you didn't either. If you want to learn more about what constitutes a healthy diet, check out the President's Council on Fitness, Sports and

Nutrition website or the Health Canada website. Both are packed full of easy-to-digest info on ways to improve your diet.

http://www.fitness.gov/eat-healthy/how-to-eat-healthy/

healthycanadians.gc.ca/eating-nutrition/healthy-eating-saine-alimentation/index-eng.php

4. Take good care of your teeth. Do a thorough job of flossing your teeth once a day, brush twice a day, and rinse with a good antiseptic mouthwash every day. Avoid sugar as much as possible too! These simple, easy-to-implement steps will drastically shift the odds in your favour for avoiding any major dental issues that will eat up piles of your hard-earned money. A great source of info and tips on the subject can be found at MouthHealthy.org (run by the American Dental Association):

mouthhealthy.org

There is also information available on the Canadian Dental Association's website:

http://www.cda-adc.ca/en/oral_health/index.asp

So did you check out those websites I showed you above? If not, do it now. I'll wait here.

The healthier your lifestyle, the less likely you are to come down with an illness that costs you a lot of money. Sure, there are no guarantees, but it can't hurt to put the odds in your favour, right?

And if, despite your best efforts, you still have the misfortune of having to take on a bunch of medical expenses, here are 14 more tips that will help you save some cash.

But first, it goes without saying that I am not suggesting you skimp on quality of treatment or put your health at risk by going to sub-par providers just to save a buck. Your health isn't worth it, and if something goes wrong, it'll cost you more in the long run. So whenever possible, choose a provider based on quality first, then use these tips to chip away at the cost.

1. Ask for a freebie if starting a new medication regimen. Doctors sometimes have samples that they can give you for free. This way, if you end up not being able to take the full course of therapy, you didn't end up wasting a bunch of money.

2. Ask your doctor if they have any manufacturer's coupons or discount cards available for your medication. Manufacturers of expensive brand name medication sometimes provide doctors with coupons or discount cards that can be used to chop the price significantly. I was able to save almost 50% on the cost of one of my prescription medications this way.

3. Find out if getting a referral to a specialist will mean you pay less money. Nowadays, it is often possible to skip straight to seeing a specialist for whatever is ailing you. But sometimes, it will cost you less if you first get a referral from your family doctor. For example, where I live, if I were to see a dermatologist without a referral, I'd have to pay 100% of the cost. But if my family doctor refers me, I pay nothing. Also, if you depend on insurance to cover the bulk of your doctor visit costs, the co-pay for a visit to a specialist is usually much higher compared to what you'd pay to see your family doctor. So before making an appointment with a pricey specialist, check first to see if you can save a few bucks by letting your family doctor handle your care.

4. Ask your doctor to prescribe a less expensive generic medication if possible. Don't make the mistake of thinking that buying generic medicine is like buying imitation Haagan Daz ice-cream. In the case of the ice cream, true, the generic imitation stuff is almost never as tasty as the brand name. But when it comes to medication, it's the active ingredient that makes the difference, and by law in North America, no matter who makes it, it has to have the advertised amount of active ingredient. For the vast majority of people, your body won't notice the difference between the generic and brand name drug — but your bank account sure will. You can save a huge amount of money by using the generic version, so at least give it a try. Say it with me now "Using generic medication is not the same as buying imitation Haagan Daz."

5. If a generic version of your medication is not available, ask for a therapeutic alternative that does have a generic. For many conditions, there is more than one first choice option for treatment. And knowing this can save you big bucks. Don't be shy; ask your doctor if there are any less costly options that will be just as effective at treating your condition.

6. Check with your pharmacist if you can save money by using a different strength of medication. Let's say you're taking a 20mg tablet once a day — it might be cheaper to take 1/2 a 40 mg tablet per day (I know, that totally defies common sense, but it is what it is.) Or let's say you're taking a 100mg tablet twice a day, it might be cheaper to take a 200mg tablet once per day. Sure, this doesn't work for every medication, but it's worth asking about just in case. You'd be shocked by the savings that can be found sometimes.

7. Ask your pharmacist if your OTC (non-prescription) medications are covered by your insurance company. You can also check directly with your insurance company. I once had over-the-counter medications that I paid cash for, and four years later found out that I could have had $500 worth per year paid for by my insurance company, if only I'd gotten a prescription for them from my doctor and had him apply for special coverage. I lost out on $2000 for nothing! Don't make the same mistake I did.

8. Stick to providers that are within your insurance company's network. Your insurance company negotiates rates with providers in the network, and if you go outside the network, you'll have to pay the difference in cost if it ends up being more expensive.

9. Check prices at different facilities. Let's say you need surgery. Did you know the cost can vary widely depending on which facility you go to? So call around and check; this simple step could save you thousands of dollars. Or let's say you sprained your ankle — odds are that you'll pay much less to be seen at a walk-in or urgent care clinic compared to a hospital emergency room. It's also worth comparing prices for things like lab work, and other diagnostic tests.

10. If you'll be paying out of pocket, let the provider know. Let's say you have a high deductible insurance policy which means there's a good chance you'll never see a dime in reimbursement from your insurance company. If you tell that to your provider, there are very high odds that they will charge you less. This tactic works around the world, everywhere from North America to Asia. When it's just some faceless corporation paying the bill, it's natural for your provider to make as much profit as possible, so they figure why not charge a bit more since "the insurance company will pay it, it's not hurting anyone." But when they know it's you personally who will foot the bill (and feel the accompanying pain of the drain on your bank account), they will often try to help you out by lowering their price.

11. Before using after-hours care, check if it'll cost extra. Seeing a doctor overnight or on weekends costs more in many locales. So for non-urgent issues, you can save money by seeing the doctor during normal business hours.

12. Claim your medical expenses on your income tax return to take advantage of any available tax breaks. There are often tax credits and refunds available to you if you save all of your medical expense receipts — this often includes expenses for dental work, eye glasses and contact lenses, physician visits, diagnostic tests, medication, and hospital stays.

13. Do your research on pricing for medical procedures ahead of time. You can get a good idea ahead of time for what a medical procedure ought to cost with the Healthcare Bluebook. This is a really cool little site that's been featured in the likes of Forbes Magazine and

The Wall Street Journal. Give it a look!

https://www.healthcarebluebook.com/

14. Ask your doctor if all of the recommended treatments are really necessary. I know, your first reaction might be to think that obviously they are necessary; otherwise, they wouldn't have suggested them. But keep in mind that for many conditions, there is more than one way to approach the problem, and often there are large price differences between the various options. For example, my husband had a sizable kidney stone and he had two options: wait and see if he could pass it naturally, or let the doctor go in and blast it with a laser so it would come out quicker. In his case, the doctor said there was currently no harm in trying to pass it on his own; this saved us big bucks, and he avoided a more invasive surgical procedure that he didn't want.

Household and Cleaning Supplies — 8 Simple Ways to Save

1. Use mild dish soap and/or plain water for simple cleaning jobs. A simple solution using only these two ingredients can be used for cleaning counters, removing greasy stains from laundry, washing fruits and vegetables, lifting stains from carpets, and loads of other things. And it's cheap. Especially if you buy a generic store brand. Obviously, you'll want to spot test first before using it on a large area of carpet or clothing, but it usually rinses out perfectly well, without leaving any damage behind.

2. Switch to florescent light bulbs. They cost the most in the short term, but because they last so much longer and use less energy than regular bulbs, in the long run they'll save you money.

3. Stock up on supplies when they go on sale. Household supplies and cleaners tend to store well, so you might as well stock up when they are being sold at a discount. If you do it right, you'll never have to pay full price again, since you'll always have enough left over to last you until the next good sale.

4. Use the generic store brand whenever possible. In most cases, the store brand will be just as good as the brand name product, for a fraction of the price.

5. Choose re-useable supplies. In the long run, it'll save you lots of cash. For example, you could choose to make the Swiffer company rich by buying their fancy Swiffer devices, with the need to buy replacement pads all the time, or you could buy a mop that doesn't require a steady stream of replacement parts and keep more of your money. Instead of using paper towels for everything, most jobs can be done with a washable rag that you reuse. For washing dishes, rather than use disposable sponges and disposable cloths, use ones that you can throw in the washing machine to freshen up and re-use.

6. Keep it simple. Rather than buy a separate cleaner for every single surface in your house, buy a multipurpose cleaner. Only buy the specialty stuff if you really need it — most of the time, a multipurpose one will do the trick and cost less over the long run. And if you can, use homemade cleaning solutions. For example, vinegar and water is a great cleaner for hard floors, baking soda makes a great gentle abrasive cleaner, and they're both dirt cheap to use. Here is a great resource for more homemade cleaning solution recipes:

www.goodhousekeeping.com/home/cleaning-organizing/make-at-home-cleaners

7. Use coffee grounds instead of expensive fridge deodorizers. Do you know when I first heard of this? They used it on the airplane when my son was motion sick and vomiting. Sorry, I know that's gross. But the thing is, when the flight attendants brought over packs of coffee grounds, it completely cancelled out any unpleasant odours in the air. Imagine what it could do for the odours in your fridge? If you prefer a scent-free option, sticking a box of baking soda in there instead is a classic solution.

8. Always measure laundry detergent. It's easy to use too much, but if you take the time to read the instructions (I know, that sounds silly for something as simple as laundry detergent, but stay with me…), you may find that you've been using much more than you really needed to. Cut down on how much you're using, and you'll save a few bucks. Why not?!

Accommodations: 4 Painless Ways to Cut Costs

Ok, so we all need a place to live, and paying for that is usually one of our biggest expenses. So here are some out of the box ideas to trim your expenses with almost no effort. Actually, these are more of a "get more money" with almost no effort strategy, but since the money you get will be used to cover your mortgage payments, it effectively means you end up using less of your own money to cover your accommodations costs.

Note: These are easiest to implement if you own the place you are living in. If you are currently renting, you'll have to obtain permission from your landlord first, or risk getting evicted in many jurisdictions.

1. Rent out a room on a long-term lease. (Double check first to make sure your home insurance permits this.)

When I was growing up, our neighbours next door rented an extra bedroom out to university students. They'd rent it out a year at a time, and if the current student wanted to move out at the end of their lease, my neighbour would rent it out to someone new for the following year. Sure, it meant sharing the rest of the house with this individual, but imagine how much easier it must have been on their finances to have an extra few hundred dollars every single month flowing in like clockwork. I also know someone who was single, and built a brand new three bedroom house as soon as he could afford a down-payment. When he moved in, he promptly rented out the two extra bedrooms to his friends. Because of the extra cash, he was able to pay down his mortgage in record time.

2. If you live in a desirable vacation area, rent out a room to travelers via a site like Airbnb.com. (Again, make sure your house insurance is compatible with this plan.)

Usually the nightly rates you can charge for a short term rental are way higher than what you'd be able to get for a long-term tenant — so if you enjoy meeting new people, and don't mind having someone new around on a regular basis, this can be a great option for reducing your costs incurred for accommodations.

And here are a couple of other ideas to consider, which will work even if you are currently renting:

3. Move into a cheaper place. Who says you have to wait until you're a middle-aged empty nester to downsize? Why not downsize now? Downsizing your accommodation expenses is an easy way to upsize your budget for other stuff — and who doesn't want more money for other stuff? If you open your mind to the possibility, I bet you'll be surprised by the options available to you. You may even kick yourself for not doing this sooner (just don't kick yourself too hard!) Downsizing does not have to mean lowering your standard of living. Most people don't really *need* all the space they have anyways, so why pay extra for it? For many people who are living paycheck to paycheck, the act of moving to a cheaper place can be the one thing that changes their finances around completely.

4. Live with roommates. So this is basically the rent out a room option above, just presented a bit differently. If you're currently renting alone, why not move into a different place, but with roommates. You could even end up getting a nicer place this way, while paying less money overall.

Bethany is currently living alone, paying $660 per month for an old studio apartment on a busy street, with shared laundry facilities in the building's basement, and basically no bells and whistles as far as amenities go. So she decides to round up a couple of friends in a similar situation, and look for a three bedroom place together. What they find astounds them! They end up renting a three bedroom apartment on a quiet street for $1350 per month (that's $450 each), and the new place is newer, has ensuite laundry, a swimming pool, and a gorgeous view of the river. Now THAT is how you lower your expenses in style.

Ben likes to live in nice new places, and he's currently paying $1100 per month for a nice one bedroom apartment with all the bells and whistles. He decides to implement my roommate strategy. Lucky for him, his cousin is also looking for a place, so they decide to be roommates. It turns out that for only $200 a month extra, they can get a two bedroom place in the same building that Ben was already living in. He is now paying only $650 per month, but still has a great apartment that he loves.

Now I know these prices will vary widely depending on where you live, but the principle behind the roommate strategy will work in many markets. So give it a go; you'll be glad you did.

Credit Card Debt: How to Save Money by Trimming Your Interest Rates

If you carry a balance on your credit cards, transfer it to a lower interest card, or a line of credit. Ok, so you know you shouldn't carry a balance on your cards, but if it's too late and you already have it, then you might as well pay as little in interest as possible while you pay it off.

Right this minute, I want you to take a look at your credit card statements and find out what the total is that you owe, and what you're paying in interest. Seriously, do it right now. I'll hang out here while you take care of that.

Got the numbers? Great! Next, contact your bank and find out if you'd qualify for a line of credit big enough to cover the expense of paying off your credit cards right now. Double check the rate of interest they'll charge you. I bet you it's way lower than what your credit card company is charging you. Bank closed right now? Then put this on your to-do list for first thing in the morning on the next business day. If they agree to give you the line of credit (you might have to go in for an appointment and speak with a loan officer personally), then take it. Now pay off all those credit cards. And do not, under any circumstances, run up a credit card balance again — if you can't trust yourself not to, then cancel the credit cards and cut them up. Problem solved. Now focus on paying off that line of credit as quick as you can.

Worst case: If you can't get a line of credit from your bank, head for Google and take a look at the competitor's credit cards on offer. Do any of them offer lower interest rates? Do you meet their cardholder financial requirements? If you do, take note of the rates and the cards that are offering them, then call your current credit card company and see if they will match it. Often they will do this if it means they get to keep you as a customer. In one phone call, you can save yourself a ton of cash with the lower rates you can get.

Worst case: If your current credit card company refuses to match the interest rates on the other cards, then apply for those better cards, transfer your balance over to the new lower rate, then cancel the old card. But before you do this, double check to see if there is a fee that you'll be charged for transferring the balance over. Only transfer your balance over if whatever fee you'll pay is offset by the savings you'll get with the new, lower interest rate.

Another really cool thing that can happen is that sometimes the new credit card will offer 0% interest for the first few months. Keep an eye out for those kinds of offers too, keeping in mind that whatever balance transfer fees you might pay must be offset by the interest savings — if not, it's not worth your time to do the transfer.

Banking Fees: 3 Easy Steps to Reduce Your Fees (Plus 4 Bonus Tips)

It's often outrageous how much money we spend in fees to access our own money at the bank. But the good news is that it's pretty easy to cut these expenses down to an absolute minimum.

1. Find out what you are paying in bank fees right now. Check out your bank statements for the past few months — how much did you pay in service fees? I'll wait here while you do that.

2. Contact your bank and find out exactly how their fee schedule works, and which plan (if any) you are currently on. For example, are you paying a flat rate every month, and if so, how many transactions does that allow? And if you go over the maximum allowed, how much are they charging you for that?

3. Change your plan to a more cost effective one. For example, Megan has a plan that charges her $12 per month and includes 50 transactions a month. But Megan makes 70 transactions per month (and it costs her an extra $0.90 per transaction above and beyond the original 50) — bringing her grand total to $30 per month in fees! She calls her bank and finds out there is another plan available for $18 per month, one that allows unlimited transactions, and she can switch plans effective immediately. This saves her $12 a month, or a total of $144 per year. I know that's not a ton of money, but I bet if someone handed you $144 cash for nothing, you wouldn't turn it down, would you? This is no different. Or to put it another way, if you spend five minutes to make that simple phone call, you just made 144 bucks for your time — best hourly wage ever!

4 Bonus Tips

1. Charge it! What if, instead of using your debit card to pay for everything, you simply charged it all to a credit card. Obviously, this means you will only buy things you need, and you will pay off your credit card in full, each and every month. But think about it: If you can do this without going hog wild and spending too much merely because you're "charging it," you'll be replacing countless little debit transactions per month with one big one (i.e., when you pay off your credit card). How much money in bank transaction fees can that save you? Tons! And, better still, find out if you qualify for a credit card that gives you a cash back bonus for your spending.

For example, in Canada, the zero-fee President's Choice Master Card gives cardholders a credit of 1% of their purchases, which can be used to buy groceries at their affiliated grocery store (and that grocery store also happens to be the cheapest one in town.)

In the United States, you can get the American Express Blue Cash Everyday Card. It gives you 3% back on grocery purchases, 2% at US gas stations and department stores, plus 1% back on other purchases.

https://www304.americanexpress.com/credit-card/blue-cash-everyday

Let's be conservative here and assume all you get back is 1%. And let's say you charge $1500 per month to your credit card. That's $180 in FREE MONEY that you'll get back every single year. And you don't have to do anything special to get it.

Credit cards get a bad rap, and rightfully so, when they encourage people to run up huge balances that they can't afford to pay back. But as you can see, if you're disciplined enough to use your credit cards wisely, you can profit from them.

2. Use only the cheapest ATM machines. Did you know that the fees you pay for using an ATM machine can vary widely? For example, banks will often give you a discount on fees if you use their own bank machines, over those that are not in their network. For example, if you bank with the Royal Bank, you will likely pay a lower transaction fee for taking out money at a Royal Bank ATM machine, compared to making a withdrawal at a random machine owned by some other company. And also, you'll notice that there are many privately owned

ATM machines that are not affiliated with any one particular bank. These kinds of machines often charge ridiculously high fees that are in addition to whatever fees your own bank will charge you. Avoid these privately owned machines whenever possible. Contact your bank today and find out if their ATM fees vary depending on what ATM machine you use.

3. Make a small number of large cash withdrawals instead of lots of small ones. For example, if you know you spend about $500 every two weeks on groceries and other household shopping expenses, why not take out $500 cash every two weeks and pay a single fee, instead of using your debit card or a series of smaller withdrawals that will each have their own fee? It adds up, and it's easy to avoid with a little bit of planning.

4. Look for a bank account that charges zero fees.

How about that, huh? It may surprise you to know that there are bank accounts available that will charge you absolutely nothing to access your money, ever.

In Canada, take a look at the President's Choice Financial Chequing Account.

www.banking.pcfinancial.ca/mkt/bankaccounts/nofeebankaccount-en.html

In the United States, take a look at the Capitol One 360 Account.

https://home.capitalone360.com

Also, do a quick google search for "no fee checking account" or "no fee chequing account" — you'll be amazed at the options that are out there!

Summing Up

You've learned a great deal of information so far that will help you to break free from living paycheck to paycheck, and get on the path to controlling your money and reaching your financial goals. You've learned:

- the most important things you can do to take control of your money
- the most common budget myths, and why you shouldn't let them stop you from making a budget
- why a budget is important in the first place, and the mindset you need to succeed at keeping one
- easy ways of making your money stretch much further
- why people fail to stick to their budget

So now that you're armed with all of that valuable information, you're ready to get to the really good part: taking control of your money once and for all by making a budget. Are you ready? Let's get to it!

Budgeting 101: How to Make a Budget

The secret to getting ahead is getting started. Mark Twain

Now that you are armed with knowledge about how a budget can help you, the common misconceptions about budgeting, and the reasons why people fail to stick to a budget, and you know the easiest ways to have more money without earning more, you're ready to start making a budget. This is the most important thing you'll ever do in taking control of your money.

You can't control what you don't understand, so it's time you learned everything about where your money is coming from, and where it's going.

In the introduction, you saw a link where you can download your own personal Money Tracker for free. It will make it super easy for you to keep track of every single penny, using your computer or laptop. And, you won't have to go through the hassle of adding up numbers on a calculator either, since the Money Tracker will do it for you.

If you haven't grabbed your free Money Tracker yet, then do it now. When you've finished, come back here. I'll wait.

Get the Money Tracker for FREE here:

http://averybreyer.com/1hr-budget-how-to-stop-living-paycheck-to-paycheck-opt-in/

The Only Tool You Need to Take Control of Your Money

You don't need anything fancy or expensive to keep track of your money. When I first started, I used a notebook, pen, and calculator. That's it. So if by some chance you can't or don't want to download the free Money Tracker, then you could always do it this way.

But adding up all those numbers by hand can be tedious (trust me, I've been there!), so you might as well take advantage of modern technology and eliminate that job. The Money Tracker is the solution. It adds up everything for you; the only thing you need to do is fill in the blanks. And, since you store all the info on your computer, you don't have to worry about a nosy third party having access to it, as you do with cloud-based budgeting tools.

And unlike budgeting apps for your smart phone, you won't be missing out on good conversation when out with friends because you're too busy entering your bills into an app on the spot, and you don't have to peck away at a miniature keyboard when you're doing it. Instead, you can do it in private, at a time that's convenient for you, on a keyboard that's big enough to actually type on!!!

Don't be fooled into thinking you need to buy some sort of fancy accounting software. It's simply not necessary, and I'm sure you can come up with better things to spend your money on.

One last thing… What you're going to read over in this chapter is the most tedious section of the entire process.

But don't let that scare you off.

It's a necessary evil if you want to live a life that's free from stressing about money. (Alright, so maybe not 100% free of money stress since that would be impossible, but I promise you that by going through this process you'll be a heck of a lot <u>more</u> free from money stress compared to NOT doing this at all!)

So get comfortable, grab something to drink, maybe a snack too, and get ready to do this. It'll be worth it.

If your mind starts to wander, take a break, go for a walk or do something to stretch your legs and clear your head — then come back and carry on from where you left off. Slow and steady wins the race and all that, right? I promise that the process gets easier once you get through this part.

How to Navigate the Money Tracker

If you're new to spreadsheets, then give this section a quick read. On the other hand, if you've had lots of experience using spreadsheets in Microsoft Excel or Open Office, then you can probably skip ahead to the next section, "How to Use the Money Tracker."

When you open the Money Tracker, you'll see that there are tabs at the lower left corner: "Month 1 Sample," "Month 1" (you fill this out) "Month 2," "Month 3," etc. You can left-click on the tabs to move between them. Try it. When you are finished, left-click on "Month 1 Sample" before you continue reading.

Also, on the bottom of the Money Tracker, next to the tabs you just clicked through, you'll see a slider bar. Hover your mouse cursor over the slider, then press and hold your left mouse button. Now slide the bar to the right along your screen — the green "Income" section and then the brown "Debt" section of the Money Tracker should come into view. Now left-click and hold your mouse cursor on the slider bar and slide it back to the right — the grey "Expenses" section should be back in view.

You can scroll down the document; you'll see that there is more room for entering data than you will ever use. Now scroll back up to the top.

Last, but not least, you'll notice that some entries in the Money Tracker have a little red dab in the upper right corner of the block. This red dab means that there is a comment associated with that entry. For example, look at the "Surplus-To-Date" box near the top; now hover your mouse over that box. You'll see a comment appear: "Red means you overspent by that amount; black means you have money left over for savings." You can do this any time you see one of those little red dabs.

Easy peasy, right? Now you're ready to move on.

How to Use the Money Tracker

The Money Tracker (or the good 'ol do-it-yourself notebook method) is key to being successful with budgeting. If you want to stop living paycheck to paycheck, the first step is figuring out exactly what is going on with your money:

- Precisely what are you spending your money on?
- How much do you earn each month?
- How much debt do you owe?
- How much of your money needs to be set aside for regular monthly payments?
- Are there any predictable expenses that you could be setting aside money for each month, such as Christmas presents, or once yearly insurance premiums?

If you follow the instructions in this chapter, you'll see that the Money Tracker will allow you to easily answer all of those questions. Once you've done that, it will become much easier to figure out exactly what you need to do in order to stop living paycheck to paycheck and start living a life where you feel confident that you'll always have enough money.

Take your time, and read over the instructions in this chapter thoroughly so you become familiar with how the Money Tracker works. As you read through the instructions in this chapter, take a good look at the "Sample" tab, and make a few test entries there to see how things work. In the next chapter, you'll start to enter your real-life data into the Money Tracker.

Yellow Section — Summary of Income, Expenses, and Monthly Surplus

All of the yellow sections are automatically calculated for you. You'll never need to enter anything in these boxes.

At the top of each month's spreadsheet, you'll see the yellow "Surplus-To-Date" and "This Month's Surplus" sections. This is where you'll see if you're making more than you're spending, and how much your savings have grown (or shrunk).

The Money Tracker will automatically calculate these figures, and instantly adjust them any time you enter something new into your income or expenses column.

"This Month's Surplus" is simply the figure you get if you subtract this month's expenses from your income. If the number here is red, it means you spent more than you earned this month. If the number is black, it means your income is more than your expenses (so far) this month.

"Surplus-to-Date" is the figure you get when you add this month's surplus to last month's surplus. If the number here is black, then you're on the right track — you're "in the black" and spending less than you earn; this figure represents the leftover money. If the number here is red, it means that since you started using the Money Tracker, you've spent this amount over and above what you've earned.

Above the grey section, you'll see your "Total Monthly Expenses." This is where the Money Tracker keeps a running tally of the expenses you've entered so far this month. Since expenses are a drain on your bank account, this figure will always be red.

Left-click the slider bar in the bottom right corner of the Money Tracker and slide it over until you see the green "Income" section. Above this green section, you'll see your "Total Monthly Income." This is where the Money Tracker keeps a running tally of the income you've entered so far this month. Since income is always a boon to your bank account, this figure will always be black.

Left-click the slider bar in the bottom right corner of the Money Tracker and slide it over once again until you see the brown "Debts" section. In this section, you'll see areas where the Money Tracker will automatically add up the total of what you owe.

Grey Section — Expenses

The grey section is where you'll keep track of all of the expenses that you run into every single month. There are sections for groceries, utility bills, rent or mortgage payments, household supplies, loan payments, discretionary spending, irregular miscellaneous expenses, and other predictable expenses.

You can change the names of the categories if you wish. But for now, I'll explain the way I use them.

Groceries: I recommend that you only use this category for food that you prepare yourself. So things like fresh produce, bread, meat, eggs, and dairy products go here. If it's been pre-cooked for you by the deli department (e.g., a ready-to-serve tray of cooked lasagna), then that belongs in the discretionary spending column. It's the more expensive way to eat (and unnecessary), so it'll help you to keep track of that kind of thing separately in case you ever need to look for easy ways to trim expenses. Obviously, there will always be some things that are borderline between prepare-yourself and pre-cooked; just use your best judgement and try to be consistent in the way you categorize things.

Utility Bills: This is where you can keep track of what you're spending on things like electricity, natural gas, and your household's water bill. You can also stick your internet, cable and telephone bills here if you like. Or put that into discretionary spending if you feel that you could skip these services in a pinch.

Rent or Mortgage Payments: Fill out how much you spend each month on your rent or mortgage payment.

Household Supplies: This is a good place to track expenses for things like toilet paper, facial tissue, household cleaners, and the like.

Loan Payments: If you have a car loan, student loan, or any other payments you make towards borrowed money, enter them here.

Discretionary Spending: This is for all the stuff that is totally optional to spend money on — stuff you can live without. Include things like eating out for dinner, buying a cup of coffee at Starbucks, gifts, going out to a movie, purchasing a video-on-demand movie, or buying a new pair of shoes simply because they were too nice to resist (as opposed to buying a pair of shoes because you truly need another), etc.

Transportation: This is where you'll track your monthly expenses for things like car repairs, gas for your car, bus fare, etc.

Other: This is where you'll put anything that is not discretionary, and is not already included elsewhere. Some of the items you'll want to include here are things like replacing a worn out pair of shoes that you can't do without. If you spent $5000 to invest in the stock market, enter this as an expense in the "other column." (When you sell, you can enter the proceeds as income.)

Take a good look over the Month 1 sample tab on the Money Tracker now. Take note of where the different kinds of expenses were placed. You'll see that some entries have a little red tag in the upper right corner of the box — hover your mouse over it and you'll see a comment that goes along with the entry. These comments offer explanatory notes about that entry.

Blue Section: Special Savings

This section tracks money you put aside for larger expenses that come up infrequently, such as Christmas presents, car repairs, once yearly insurance premiums, etc.

- The "Description" column is for you to enter a brief description of the expense.
- The "Amount" column is where you'll fill out how much money you'll have to put aside each month. (The total yearly cost divided by 12.)
- The "Spent" column is for tracking how much money you've spent on this category in the year so far.
- The "Total" column is automatically calculated for you — it represents the amount of money you currently have saved up for this particular expense.

VERY IMPORTANT: The blue special savings section will only be able to add up your savings in each category correctly if you always enter your savings descriptions in the same spot each and every month. Take a look at the "Month 1 Sample" tab on the Money Tracker. Do you see how "Retirement" is in the third slot on the far left of the Special Savings section?

Let's pretend that whatever is in the Month 1 sample tab is in your Month 1 tab.

If that were the case, you can never put something else in that slot because the Money Tracker will always think it's for "Retirement." So if you were to have "Retirement" there in Month 1, and in Month 2, you decide to put "Christmas" on the third slot on the far left of the Special Savings section, the Money Tracker will not be able to total the amount of money you have saved up towards that expense correctly. If you have any trouble with this, contact me via my website, www.averybreyer.com/contact, and I'll be glad to help you figure it out!

Example: Let's use car maintenance and repairs as an example. Say you estimate that you usually spend about $2400 per year on car maintenance and repairs. Under the "Description" column, you might enter "Car Repairs." Under the "Amount" column, you should enter "$200" ($2400 divided by 12 months). Let's say you start saving for this in Month 1 of your Money Tracker.

In Month 3, your car requires some minor maintenance which costs you $150. If you've been putting aside $200 per month for car maintenance, Month 3 of your Money Tracker will show the following:

- $200 in the "Amount" column
- $150 in the "Spent" column
- $450 in the "Total column

This reflects the fact that you've saved $200 per month for three months ($600), then spent $150 of that money, leaving you with $450 remaining in your car maintenance and repairs fund.

Example: What to do if you spend more than you had saved up for one of your special savings categories:

Let's say you budgeted $2400 per year for car maintenance and repairs, so you're putting aside $200 per month for this. After only six months of saving up ($1200 in your car repair fund), you end up facing an unexpectedly large repair bill of $2000.

What I recommend that you do is simply enter $1200 in the "Spent" column of your car maintenance category in the blue "Special Expenses" section. Then enter the leftover $800 ($2000-$800) in your "Other" section of the grey "Expenses" section. This way, the unanticipated extra spending will automatically be subtracted from your monthly surplus.

Think of all of the expenses that are not discretionary and only come up infrequently, such as once per year insurance premiums and potentially large car maintenance and repair bills. Jot them down, along with what you estimate they will cost you in a one year period. Divide the yearly figures by 12, and enter your data into the blue "Special Expenses" section of the "Month 1" tab on your Money Tracker. (Do not use the "Month 1 Sample" tab for this; use the plain "Month 1" tab.)

Green Section: Income

Of course, knowing what you're spending your money on is only half the job. You also need to have a very good idea as to how much money is coming into your bank account each month.

The green section of the Money Tracker is where you'll keep track of this. You'll enter all sources of income including things like employment income, child or spousal support, government cheques, investment income, etc.

Brown Section: Debts

Use the slider bar at the bottom of the Money Tracker to scroll to the right, past the green Income section. You should see the brown Debt section now.

The purpose of this section is to allow you to see at a glance how much money you owe. A lot of people hate looking at this section and find it depressing. But the thing is, if you stick your head in the sand

and pretend it doesn't exist, you have no hope of managing this part of your life appropriately. So be brave, and face this head on.

You need to know what you owe so you can come up with a workable plan to deal with it. Knowledge is power, my friend!

Ready?

Ok. The top portion is where you'll keep track of any debts you have for which there is no minimum monthly payment owed. So let's say you are a student with student loans, which do not need to be paid back until after graduation. This is where you will keep track of the balance owing for this.

The bottom portion is where you'll keep track of any debts you have for which there IS a minimum monthly payment. This could include things such as your mortgage or a car loan. If you have credit card debt that you do NOT pay off in full each month, then enter that in here too (since presumably your credit card company will set a minimum monthly payment for you, right?).

Both of these sections have a spot to enter your borrowing limit. This is important information to know, especially if you are currently in a situation where you need to keep adding to your debt. For example, you don't want to be caught by surprise some day and find that you can't borrow any more money against your line of credit if you've been depending on that ability to survive — it's better to see it coming from a mile away, so you can better prepare for it.

These sections also have a place for you to track the interest rate. If you are able to start paying down these debts faster than the minimum required of you, you'll use the interest rate charged to determine which loan should be paid off first — you'll want to make it a priority to pay off the loans with the highest interest rates.

Once a month, you should enter the current interest rate for whatever debts you are still carrying, and the amount you owe as of the first of that month. You can refer to the previous month's information to ensure you don't forget anything.

Special Circumstances

Students and Summer Jobs

What if I'm a student and some or all of my "income" is from student loans?

Good question! Here is what I recommend. Let's say you live off $20,000 in student loans per year. Then take that, divide it by 12, and you'll have an "income" from student loans of $1666.00 per month. If you also have a monthly payment that you need to make on the loan, then enter that amount in the loan column.

What if I I'm a student and I only work for four months of the year when I'm off school for the summer?

You probably have a pretty good idea of what you will make over the summer, right? So, at the start of your summer job, take the total amount you estimate that you'll make over the four months you'll be working, and divide it evenly over the 12 month year. So if you think you'll make $12,000 over the four months that you are working in the summer, then you can average that out over the entire year and enter an "income" of $1000 per month.

Let's say summer is over and you made $1200 more than what you originally though you would. Then you can do one of two things. You can add that in as a lump sum to the income for this month. Or, you can figure out how many months are left in this 12 month period and divide that sum evenly between them, making an entry for the appropriate amount in each of the remaining monthly tabs.

Let's say summer is over and you made $500 less than you originally thought you would. Then you can either enter an income figure of

-500 in this month's income section, or, divide the $500 by the number of months left in this 12 month period, and enter a negative figure for each of those.

Windfalls

What if I receive a $20,000 inheritance this year? How do I track it?

Since this is a one-time deal, I recommend that you simply add it to your income for the current month — the Money Tracker will add it onto your surplus-to-date. In the notes section of the Money Tracker for this month, you can mention that the reason for this month's large surplus is because of that inheritance.

Large Withdrawals from Surplus

My surplus-to-date is getting to the point where I can afford to withdraw a nice chunk of it to invest for retirement. How do I track this?

Let's say you have $5000 that you'd like to transfer into your retirement investment or savings account. Simply mark that down as -5000 in the "other" expenses column. The money tracker will automatically account for this by decreasing your surplus-to-date accordingly. In the notes section of the Money Tracker for this month, you can mention that the reason this month's surplus is negative is because of that withdrawal.

Action Steps:

1. Download your Money Tracker and learn how to use it.
2. Choose your budget start date.

Month 1: Find Out Where You Stand

Truth can stand by itself. Thomas Jefferson

Now you get to the most important part. You know, the part where you figure out where you stand. If you want to stop living paycheck to paycheck, it's really important that you are totally honest when doing the work in this chapter. And once you do, you'll see how much easier it becomes to take control and figure out a low-stress budgetary plan that will work for you in Month 2.

To keep things simple, I suggest you start this on the first of the next month.

That being said, if you're hungry to start NOW, then that'll work too — just be sure to remember what day of the month you started on, so you can be consistent every month. For example, if you start on the 12th of this month, then you have to start on the 12th of every month from now on.

Your Mission for the First Month

Sure, you could start making a "budget" right now, but what use would THAT be if you have absolutely no idea how much you spend on necessities like groceries, utilities, and transportation, right?

So, the first part of your mission for this month, should you choose to accept it, is to use the Money Tracker to track every single penny you spend, and every single penny you earn. Now this might sound like a lot of work, but if you do it right, I promise you, it's not.

Remember, once you have everything set up, it won't take you more than about one hour per month, or 15 minutes a week, to do this.

Step 1: Track Your Spending

Grab a jar, an old shoebox, or anything large enough to stuff your receipts in. Then stick a pen and paper near it.

From now on, every single time you buy something, no matter how small, you're going to save the receipt and stick it in there.

Once a week, you will take those receipts, and enter them into the grey Expenses section of the Money Tracker.

If you buy something online (and therefore don't have a paper receipt), you can either enter it in the Money Tracker right when you make the purchase, or jot down the details and enter it in the Money Tracker along with all your paper receipts once a week. Do the same for any utility bills that you pay online.

Don't forget: If you have any regular monthly payments such as car loans, mortgage, or rent to pay, be sure to enter those into the grey expense section of the Money Tracker also.

Step 2: Track Your Earnings

Every single time you get a paycheque, a government cheque (for example, a monthly benefit cheque), or any other source of income, mark it down in the green Income section of your Money Tracker. Or save the cheque stub showing the amount of money received, and enter the info into the green Income section of the Money Tracker once a week along with your spending receipts.

Also, take a look at how much money you currently have in your bank account. Whatever money you have saved up in your bank account should be added to the green Income section of your Money Tracker. Under Description, enter something like "Month 1 starting cash." This is a one-time job that you need to do in order to take into account any extra cash you have sitting around.

Step 3: Track Your Debts

Knowing how much money you owe is critical to taking control of your money and reaching your financial goals. It can be scary or disheartening to take a hard look at how much money you owe, but you are far more likely to be able to pay it off once you know what you're dealing with. So be brave, take a deep breath, and go for it.

I always say, if you keep your head in the sand, you don't know where the kick's coming from. Herbie Mann

Now the first step in tracking your debts is to ask yourself a few questions:

Do I have any credit card debt or loans that I should pay off? How much do I owe for each? Is there a minimum monthly payment? If so, how much is it?

Add any debts that do NOT have a minimum monthly payment, such as a line of credit, to the top section of the brown debt area in the Money Tracker. Fill in the appropriate blanks.

Add any debts that DO have a minimum monthly payment, such as a car loan, to the bottom section of the brown area in the Money Tracker. Fill in the appropriate blanks. After that, enter the minimum monthly payment required into the Loan Payment area of the grey Expenses section.

See the positive possibilities. Redirect the substantial energy of your frustration and turn it into positive, effective, unstoppable determination. Ralph Marston.

Whatever the amount of debt that you owe, have faith in your abilities to successfully deal with it. Remember, you are only on Month 1 of your budgeting journey. But once you have collected all of the data on your spending and earnings, you can get started in figuring out how to pay it down. With patience and time, you can get your finances under control.

Step 4: Come Up With an Income and Spending Backup Plan

You need to have a plan B in case plan A doesn't work out. Add an extra layer of protection to your ability to stick to your budget and stop living paycheck to paycheck by giving some thought to the following questions:

- If I had to, could I earn more money? Do I have time to work more hours, get a second job, or start a business on the side, yet still meet all of my other obligations?
- How can I cut down on my expenses? Use some of the things you read about in previous chapters to spark some ideas.

Be really honest with yourself when answering those questions. You may not WANT to, but COULD you, if necessary? This is the time for giving yourself a bit of tough love.

Having the answers to these questions mapped out in advance gives you a quick-action plan to implement now that can help you stop living paycheck to paycheck.

And later on, once you've dug yourself out of whatever financial hole you're in now, these backup plans will help a lot in the event that you are ever blindsided by an unexpected income cut, or a huge expense that catches you by surprise. This action plan is particularly important to have in place when you're in that vulnerable budgetary stage of not having your emergency fund saved up yet. Or maybe you did have an emergency fund set up, but it's been depleted and you have to start saving it up all over again.

5. Track Your Savings Goals:

Your first priority is to figure out how much money you need to be setting aside each month for predictable expenses. Get started by asking yourself the following question:

What are the expenses that I know will come up from time to time, that I should be saving up for in advance? (Include things that *are* necessary, such as your annual insurance payments, for example.) What is the deadline by which I absolutely must have this money?

Note: Saving up for expenses that don't come up on a regular basis is a step that a lot of people miss, and the source of a lot of budget-destroying expenses. But it doesn't have to be that way if you plan for them in advance.

Here is a list of common expenses that people include here:

- Christmas presents
- Car insurance (if you pay it once a year, rather than monthly)
- Retirement savings
- Life Insurance
- Car repairs
- Savings for a house down-payment
- Savings for supplies for a new baby
- Savings for a vacation

- Savings for your emergency fund

Since it's often hard to think of absolutely everything in one sitting, I recommend you spend 15-30 minutes on this today, then leave it for a day or two. When you come back to it, odds are you'll have thought of more items to add to your answers. Continue to add to this list over the month, whenever something new comes to mind that needs to be included here.

Let's say you spend about $1200 on Christmas presents each year. That means you have to put aside $100 per month for that ($1200 divided by 12 months), so enter $100 in the Amount column of the blue Special Expenses section, along with a brief description of what that money is for in the "description" column.

Do you own a car? We all know they have a nasty habit of breaking down once in a while, so put aside some money for that too — make your best guess on how much you spend per year on maintenance and repairs for your car (e.g., $2000 per year), divide that figure by 12 ($166), and enter that figure in the "amount" column of the Money Tracker ($166 for this example).

Maybe you'd like to take a really nice vacation two years from now, so you budget $5000 for it. You'll need to set aside $208.33 per month ($5000 divided by 24 months).

Do you have an emergency fund set aside yet? Ideally, you should have the cash saved up to sustain you for six months in case you lose your main source of income. You don't have to save up the money for this overnight, but do start putting aside money for this right now.

At the end of this month, you'll have a good idea of what your monthly expenses are. Once you have that figure, you can multiply it by six to figure out what your target emergency fund should amount to.

So if you spend $3000 per month after all taxes and deductions, your goal will be to have access to an $18000 emergency fund. To save that up over 24 months, you'd need to put aside $750 per month for the next two years. Too much money to put aside each month? Then save it up over three years (36 months), and the amount you need to set aside each month drops to only $500. Still too much money? No problem! Simply save it up over a longer period of time then. The point is to get started. Remember, any amount saved up is better than nothing, and as long as you stick with this, eventually you'll end up with your stash of emergency cash!

Summing Up on the Savings Thing

To start with, only enter those items that you MUST save for in the money tracker, such as your emergency fund — you should take care of your NEEDS first. Save all the "wants," such as that nice vacation you'd like to take, until after the end of this month, when you'll have a better idea as to whether or not you can afford to put money aside for them. If you can afford them, go ahead and add the savings for these items to the Special Savings section. If you can't, then tuck them away in your memory for now; you can always add them in future as your financial situation improves.

Step 6: Figure Out What Your Debt and Lifestyle Goals Are

The last part of your mission for this month is to decide on what you want your money to accomplish for you over the long term, as far as debt and lifestyle are concerned.

To live is to choose. But to choose well, you must know who you are and what you stand for, where you want to go and why you want to get there. Kofi Annan

I can tell you that you ought to save 'x' percentage of your income, or that you need to spend 'x' percentage or less of your income on housing. Or I could say you need to be setting aside 'x' percentage of your income on savings for retirement. (But what if right now, you're a student who is subsisting 100% on student loans and saving for retirement isn't the best use of your money right now? Heck, what if you're already retired and merely need to ensure that your monthly income covers your expenses?)

The point is, we're all different, and there is no such thing as a one-size-fits-all guideline on what a person should be spending their money on.

So this is where you come in.

You need to decide on what kind of lifestyle you want to work towards, and decide on what you want to do about any debt that you have. Don't rush it; it'll take time. To help you out, I've listed some questions below to get you started. Let's start with debt, and save the best, lifestyle goals, for last!

Debt Goals

Get started by asking yourself the following questions:

- Would I like to pay off my debt and loans faster?
- Will they allow me to make a larger monthly payment compared to what I am currently paying?
- Are there any extra charges I'll have to pay (penalty fees) for paying down my loan ahead of schedule?
- Is there a way for me to pay a lower interest rate on my debts? (e.g., If you have a mortgage, contact a mortgage broker to see if your mortgage rates can be lowered. If you are carrying credit card debt that you do not pay off in full each month, contact your bank to see if you can consolidate your credit card debts into a single low interest loan.)

Keep the answers to these questions in mind for Month 2, when you'll be solidifying your plans for dealing with your debts.

Lifestyle Goals

Get started by asking yourself the following questions:

- What is the lifestyle that I want to have, and how much money will it cost me to live it?
- How much time am I willing to commit to obtaining the money for the lifestyle I want?
- Would it be worth it to me to spend less money and downsize my lifestyle, so I don't have to work as hard or as long?

Lifestyle goals are a biggie. You've got to figure out what you want badly enough to make it worth the effort it'll take to get it.

I love the idea of working really hard and ending up with a multimillion dollar business that supports a really lavish lifestyle, but I'm not willing to work 80 hours a week for years, missing out on time with my family or time spent on hobbies I love to get it. So I've scratched that potential goal off my to-do list. I can be perfectly happy living a simple, less costly lifestyle anyhow.

On the other hand, it was worth it to me back in my university days (prior to having my kids) to work not only over the summer, but on weekends during the school year to pay my tuition (which meant between my studies and work, I was putting in 80 hour weeks). I lived this way for six years in order to graduate owing less than $2000 to my parents, which I was able to quickly pay off once I started working in the career I had trained for. It was short-term pain for long-term gain, and gave me a nice lifestyle as a new graduate since I wasn't saddled with a ton of debt. And sure, it would have been more fun to work less and party more in my school days, and it would have been more fun to go to a prestigious university far from home, pricey tuition be damned — but I wanted to avoid massive student loan debt when I graduated more than I wanted those other things, so the sacrifice was worth it.

I'm not saying these examples are the right or wrong way to look at things, but what I am saying is that you need to figure out which of your goals are worth the effort to you personally, and which ones are simply not worth the trade off in time and effort. What's "worth the effort" to me, might be different for you, and that's ok — don't let anyone tell you otherwise. You know yourself best!

Also keep in mind that just because a goal is not a good fit with your priorities in life right now doesn't mean you can't put them on the to-do list for the day that your circumstances change. So don't get too bummed out if there is something you really want to accomplish that you simply can't afford right now. Even for those goals that you can't tackle right now, you can still set yourself up to maximize the chances of reaching them later.

For example, if you have a goal of buying a house one day, and you're currently deep in credit card or student loan debt, saving up for a down payment on that house may be unrealistic at this point in time.

But.

You can start setting yourself up today for reaching the goal of buying a house later. Do everything within your power to fix a bad credit score or maintain a good one (since banks don't like to lend money to people with bad credit). Do everything within your power to pay down your loans as quickly as possible. Live as frugally as you can, without making yourself miserable, so you have more money to pay down your debt today. Once you pay off that loan, you'll be able to more easily save up that down payment and afford the mortgage payments on the house you want.

Or maybe you have a less costly goal — perhaps all you want is to be able to afford a vacation to a beautiful island in the Caribbean. The same principles apply. Do what you can today to set your life up in such a way that it will be as easy as possible later to save up the money needed to make this dream come true.

Take some time now to give these things some thought. Decide on which lifestyle goals are worth the effort to work towards now, and which ones you'll put off until a more suitable time in your life. And don't worry if you are unsure about whether or not you can afford to pursue some of your goals now. At the start of Month 2, you'll have a better idea of what you can, and can't, afford to do.

Action Steps:

1. Track your spending.
2. Track your income.
3. Track your debts.
4. Come up with an income and spending backup plan.
5. Track your savings goals.
6. Figure out your debt and lifestyle goals.

Month 2: This is the Part Where You Take Control of Your Money

Money is a great servant but a bad master. Francis
Bacon

Are you dying of suspense, wondering where you stand as far as your spending goes? Let's put an end to the suspense and find out how you're doing financially after Month 1. Then you can put together the first draft of a workable plan for your money that will take you from where you are now to where you <u>want</u> to be — a life that's free of worries about money (well, as free of worries as possible anyhow). I'll also share with you the simple tip that is proven to dramatically increase your chances of getting there.

Your Mission for the Second Month

Your mission, if you choose to accept it, begins on day one of Month 2. You're going to be brutally honest with yourself about your spending habits and income, then put together a detailed plan that will maximize your odds of reaching your financial goals. I recommend you set aside a few hours for this.

(Setting it up takes time, but it'll be worth it! And don't forget — once you finish all of the prep work, this whole thing will take no more than 15 minutes a week to maintain.)

You're going to look over how much money you spent last month (and what you spent it on), then optimize your spending and ability to bring in an income so that you are no longer living paycheck to paycheck. Then, you're going to start to prioritize your goals and figure out which ones you are going to start saving for now, and which ones you will work on sometime in the future.

The Simple Trick That is Proven to Dramatically Increase Your Chances of Achieving Your Goals

You can dramatically increase your odds of achieving your goals if you do this one simple thing: Formulate a plan for achieving them that states what you are going to do and when you will do it.

Why We Know This Works

Social scientists have proven that people who not only write down their goals, but formulate a plan to achieve them, have a much higher chance of reaching their goals compared to those who simply set them.

In addition, clearly stating how and when you will take action to achieve your goal can reduce the ability of your past behaviour to predict future behaviour. In other words, if you've always been terrible at managing your money, it doesn't mean you'll always be that way. You can change — if you first figure out what steps you need to take in order to do so, and when you will take them.

There are many studies that prove this. I won't bore you with them all, but here are a couple of examples.

1. Researchers found that women who said they would perform regular breast self-examinations only did it 53% of the time. However, women who also stated when and where they would do the self-exams did it 100% of the time. (Source)[2]
2. Researchers found that people who had a goal to eat more healthy were way more likely to actually follow through on it if they first figured out exactly how (and when) they would do it. (Source)[3]

The results are not all that surprising if you think about it. Those who formulate a detailed plan give themselves an easy-to-follow roadmap to success. Those who don't formulate a plan end up meandering along in an often random fashion, easily getting sidetracked.

Time for Your Reality Check

Alright, you've done a great job of tracking your spending and income for Month 1. Now it's time to figure out how to use what you've got to stop living a stressful paycheck-to-paycheck-lifestyle, and instead, to set yourself up for a life of more abundance. A life of more abundance doesn't have to mean you're going to jump into some get rich quick scheme. But by strategically managing your money, you'll be able to ensure you have enough money to pay for the things that are important to you. And that is the brand of abundance I teach.

You're going to start by figuring out if you are earning more, or less, than you are spending each month; then you are going to come up with a personalized action plan to dramatically improve your financial situation.

How To Put Together Your Personal Action Plan (a.k.a. Your Budget)

Whether you spent more, or less, than you earned last month, this book is going to help you figure out the best way to handle your money going forward. This section is divided into two parts:

1) What to Do If You Spent MORE Than You Earned in Month 1
2) What to Do if You Spent LESS Than You Earned in Month 1

Regardless of which category you fall into, I recommend you read over both of them since no matter what your situation is, they each contain information that could be useful to you as you strive to stop living paycheck to paycheck.

The Most Important Question You Need to Ask Yourself This Month

Did you spend more, or less, than you earned?

Regardless of what your answer is, I'll give you some ideas in the next section for how to handle your situation in a way that maximizes your odds of enjoying the life you want, free of worries about money.

Are you ready? Then let's get started!

Now take a look at "This Month's Surplus" for Month 1 in your Money Tracker. If it's a negative number, you're spending more than you earned last month. No one wants to end up in this situation, but it can happen to the best of us, so don't waste time beating yourself up about it, ok? Instead, take action to fix it. Let's get started then, shall we?

What to Do If You Spent More Than You Earned in Month 1

The next question you need to ask yourself is whether or not you only fell into this category due to a large expense that only comes up once in a while, but is predictable (for example, a once yearly insurance premium payment, or a car repair), versus something easily avoidable such as going on one too many shopping sprees. Or did you only fall into this category because you were temporarily without a job, but now you are employed again?

Assess Temporary Causes of Lack of Funds

If it turns out that your overspending was due to a one-off large expense, or a now-fixed income generation issue, no worries. But you do need to decide if this is something that is likely to come up again.

For example, car maintenance and repairs or once yearly insurance premium payments are likely to recur, right? If that's the case, then double check to see if you've accounted for those in the blue Special Savings Section of your Money Tracker. If you haven't already accounted for this situation there, then do so now. I'll wait. Remember to estimate what you're likely to spend on this expense in a 12 month period, then divide that number by 12 to figure out how much money you need to be setting aside each month for it.

Is your job seasonal, so you always end up with no money coming in at a certain time of year? Can you set aside extra money during the part of the year that you are employed, to sustain you when you are unemployed? (Tip: You can put money aside for this in the blue Special Savings section of the Money Tracker.) If you can't afford to do this, then you'll need to either cut your expenses, or increase your income. Consider your options, and make a plan. It doesn't have to be perfect, or guaranteed to work, so don't let fear of failure stop you from trying your best. Remember, a budget is a constant work in progress, and you can adjust it based on what you learn about what works for you and what doesn't.

Do you have any other large expenses in Month 1 that you should be saving for in the Special Savings category? Look for them now, then make sure that you are putting aside money for them each month in the Special Savings category from now on.

Cut Expenses

Now take a look at the grey Expenses section of your Money Tracker. Take 5-10 minutes and scan over your expenses from Month 1. Think to yourself, "How many of those expenses could easily be cut down or eliminated?" Start by cutting out those expenses for things that you'll notice the least. The Discretionary Spending area usually contains the easiest stuff to cut out.

Next, use the tips in the chapter "How to Trim Your Expenses With (Almost) No Effort," to see how much further you can reduce your spending. The idea here is to trim your expenses in the least painful way possible. You might as well start with the easiest ways first, right? If those are not enough, you can play hardball and start to cut your expenses more aggressively.

Now run the numbers again as if in Month 1 you'd already made these cuts to your spending, using the BUDGET TESTING sheet on the Money Tracker. Enter in your green income, grey expenses, and blue special savings requirements, and see how the numbers work out. You might have to make some rough guesses here regarding the amount of money you'll be able to save, and it's ok to guess. You'll fine-tune your actions after seeing the results of these cuts when you look over your numbers again next month.

Are you still spending more than you earn? Would the "This Month's Surplus" figure still be negative if you had trimmed those expenses down?

If you need to make more cuts to your expenses, then it's time to play hardball and be a bit ruthless with the cutting. This next section will help you do that.

First, if you own a car, consider how much money you'd save by selling your car and taking public transit instead. You'd have no car payments, no car insurance premiums to pay, and zero repair and maintenance bills. The savings are typically enormous if you can forego car ownership.

Use the "Budget Testing" sheet on the Money Tracker to see what your finances would look like if you did this. I'm not saying you have to choose this option, but it's in your best interest to at least see for yourself how this action would affect your finances.

Next, take a hard look at your choice of accommodations and what it's costing you. If you own your own home, consider things like renting out a room to make more money, or selling your home and buying something less expensive. If you're renting, consider moving into a less expensive place, or getting a roommate to cut costs.

Use the "Budget Testing" sheet on the Money Tracker to see what your finances might look like if you implemented any of those changes. Consider what would happen if you combined a few of these changes to turbo-charge the savings: Why not move into a less expensive place *and* rent out a room for extra money?

Lastly, take a second look at every single thing you spend your money on, and give some serious thought to whether or not you can cut any of them out, or at least reduce their cost. Here are some examples of the kinds of things you should think about:

- Maybe you don't *need* that expensive cell phone plan. Try switching to a cheap pay-as-you-go plan for emergency use only, and use your less costly landline for the rest of your calls.
- Perhaps you can forgo internet service where you live, and use the internet for free at your local library.
- Do you *really* need a monthly subscription for cable television? Many television shows can be watched for free online on the television network's website.
- Can you make less expensive grocery choices? Eating local foods (versus specialty imported items) and cooking from scratch (rather than purchasing ready-to-eat meals) are usually great money savers.

- Can you save on heating costs by lowering the temperature on the thermostat by a few degrees? Can you save on air-conditioning costs by raising the thermostat setting a couple of degrees or running a fan instead?

Now go through your list of money-saving ideas and choose whatever combination of them you like and that will bring your spending to a level that is less than the income you bring in. And don't forget: If it feels like you are sacrificing a lot to do this, it doesn't mean things will always be this way. Think of it as short-term pain for long-term gain. It'll be worth it; trust me.

Right now, you're stressed out and worried each month about whether or not you'll have enough money to pay the bills, it's embarrassing when you end up having to pay your bills late, your savings account often doesn't have enough money in it (or worse, is empty!), and you're ashamed because you don't want your family and friends to know how bad your finances are, right?

Imagine how great you're going to feel when you no longer have to scramble to find the money for things, you can always pay your bills on time, your credit score is going up and the banks are begging for your business. That is your prize for making the tough decisions, for tackling your financial problems head on, and doing what needs to be done to get your life back on track. Keep your eye on the prize, and it can be yours as long as you're willing to do the work required to get it.

Earn More Money

After considering ways in which you might cut down your expenses, it's time to figure out if it's possible for you to earn more money.

- Are you underpaid at your current job? If so, maybe now is a good time to start sending out resumes so you can find a job that pays you what you're worth.
- Can you get a second job on the side?
- Can you start one of those home-based businesses with low

start-up costs?

- Do you possess specialty knowledge or training that people will pay to have access to?
- Are you stuck in a dead-end, low-wage career path? Maybe it will be more cost-effective in the long run to cut your expenses down to an absolute minimum so you can afford to re-train for a different job entirely (assuming you choose one that not only pays better, but is highly in demand.)

For most people, using the strategies above will bring your spending and income back into balance.

And what if you are one of the few for whom this does not bring you 100% to where you'd like to be financially? At the very least, you'll have improved your situation compared to how it was before. But maybe you can still do better.

Go back over my expense cutting ideas to make sure you haven't missed any that will help you.

Think again about ways you can earn more money — are there any ideas that you may have overlooked?

Consider whether or not you could move in with family or friends until you get back on your feet.

Consider more drastic options like moving to a locale with a cheaper cost of living.

For example, many retired people find that their pensions aren't high enough to fund the lifestyle that they want, so they move to tropical locales like Panama or Costa Rica and live out their life in luxury that they simply couldn't afford back home. Adventurous people of all ages in dead-end jobs have reinvented themselves teaching English overseas in countries with a low cost of living. Heck, entire families have left everything behind to be nomadic and travel through low-cost countries and now sustain themselves via freelance work. Think outside the box!

(If you're seriously interested in the possibilities for moving out of the country to lower your living costs, then I highly recommend that you read International Living Magazine. This is a specialty publication that writes about countries around the world where you can get the best bang for your buck! Although their target market is retirees, there are nuggets of wisdom in there that will apply to people of every age.)

http://internationalliving.com/customer-dashboard/international-living-magazine/

Leaving the country is too extreme for you? No problem! Then check out other neighbourhoods that are more affordable, nearby towns and cities, or even a completely different state or province!

And remember, just because things are the way they are now, doesn't mean they will always be that way. Keep your eyes and ears open for new opportunities to save money, or earn more. Going through this process will leave you better prepared to take full advantage of any future opportunities that are in line with your goals. Whatever you do, don't give up on finding a budget that works for you! Some people are lucky and figure it out in a month; other people take a year to get everything figured out. It doesn't matter how long it takes, all that matters is that you get there eventually.

What to Do if You Spent Less Than You Earned in Month 1

If you spent less than you earned in Month 1, you are in an excellent starting position. Well done, my friend!

But hey, there might be a few things you're overlooking — things that are slowing down the progress you're making towards reaching your financial goals and being fully in control of your money. Let's fix that.

Go through the same process you would have if you were spending more than you earned, and take a look at whether or not there are any expenses you can cut out. Also give some thought as to whether or not you can earn more money. This will be important for the next section on goal setting.

Goal Setting

Now that you have an idea of how much you can reasonably cut your expenses, and how much additional earning potential you have, it's time to take a look at goals beyond just not living paycheck to paycheck.

Earlier in this chapter, you read about the simple trick that dramatically increases your chances of reaching your goals: Plan how and when you will take action to get yourself there.

You're going to do that right now. Think back to the list of financial goals you came up with in the previous chapter. Decide which ones are a priority right now and start with those. Remember to set aside money for things that need to be saved up for in advance by using the blue Special Savings section of the Money Tracker. And make saving up an emergency fund a high priority once you've figured out how to pay for your day-to-day needs.

This is the fun part — you get to choose what goals are truly important to you, and make a plan that will work for reaching them.

Be a force to be reckoned with as you pursue your goals with vigour and purpose. Do not give up, keep your eye on the prize, and use all of the skills you have learned to do everything within your power to create the life you want. Whether you have to cut your spending, or earn more money, once you know which financial goals are most important to you, and you have a plan to reach them, it becomes easier than ever to make it happen.

And remember, for those goals that aren't practical to save for right now, you can set yourself up such that it's easier to reach those goals in the future, when the time is right.

Celebrate the Small Wins

One of the things that will be key to your success in reaching your goals is to celebrate the small wins. But many of your financial goals could take years. So be sure to keep your motivation up by celebrating every single milestone you reach on the path to your final goal.

- When you put together a budget that you can live with — celebrate it!
- When you figure out how and when you will set aside a nice chunk of money each month towards your goal, give yourself a pat on the back for a job well done.
- Did you save up 25% of the money you need for your goal? 50%? 75%? Celebrate it!
- Did you figure out a way to attain a financial goal that you'd previously thought was impossible? Celebrate it!

Do you get the idea? Because if you don't savour the small wins, getting your financial life in order can seem like a long, thankless process. Celebrating the small wins along the way will make your journey a lot easier and more enjoyable.

Use Month 2 to Improve Upon Your Results from Month 1

Now that you have a plan, it's time to put it into action, ideally by day two of Month 2. If your other commitments prevent you from doing the exercises in this chapter so early in the month, so be it. Don't worry about it, just do it as soon as you can. Worst case, you might have to wait until the end of Month 3 to see the results of any changes you've made. All that matters is that you make the changes and monitor the results.

Action Steps:

1. Figure out what actions you need to take in order to reach your financial goals, and when you will take them.
2. Starting right now, celebrate the small wins along the way as you strive to reach your financial goals.
3. Continue to save all of your receipts and spend 15 minutes a week entering your income and spending into the Money Tracker.

Month 3 and Beyond: How to Stay on Track

Patience, persistence and perspiration make an unbeatable combination for success. Napoleon Hill

This chapter is short and sweet. Heck, after all your hard work in Month 1 and 2, you deserve a break!

So here's the deal. From here on out, it's all about keeping tabs on your spending, consistently filling out the Money Tracker, and making adjustments to your budget as needed.

Remember, a budget is not set in stone. If your circumstances change, don't hesitate to adjust your budget accordingly.

Sticking with this process over the long term will maximize your odds of financial health, eliminate the stress that comes with not planning ahead, and dramatically increase the odds that you will reach your financial goals. From now on, you will control your money, rather than the other way around!

Dealing with Setbacks

As you know, setbacks are an unavoidable part of life. But one of the things that sets successful people apart from those who are not is how they deal with failure. Successful people do not let failure stop them, and neither should you.

Failures, repeated failures, are finger posts on the road to achievement. One fails forward toward success. C. S. Lewis

Albert Einstein had difficulty learning as a child, yet went on to to win a Nobel Prize in physics. His discoveries are now included in school textbooks around the world!

Winston Churchill was estranged from his political party for 20 years, yet he still succeeded in getting elected as Prime Minister, and is commonly thought of as one of the greatest wartime leaders of his century.

Never forget that the most successful people among us have had some spectacular failures; failing is a normal part of the journey on the road to success. Failure makes your future self better, and the lessons you learn from your failures can be the keys to greater success than you ever thought possible.

Ignore the naysayers (including your critical inner voice), and forge ahead. Always remember that you can do this as long as you stick with it!

Important Things to Remember

- This budget of yours is a work in progress, and it's normal for it to require adjustments from time to time.
- Continue to prioritize your financial goals.
- Stick with this for a minimum of 12 months.

The bulk of your work was finished in the first two months. From here on out, all you have to do is stick to your plan, make adjustments as needed if your income or unavoidable expenses change, and carry on with spending only 15 minutes a week (one hour per month) tracking your spending and income in order to ensure that you stay on track. You're on easy street now!

As you reach old goals, it'll be possible to add new goals to your list of things to save for. Make adjustments to your budget accordingly.

As you learned in chapter 5, the longer you stick with a new habit, in this case, budgeting, the easier it becomes to stick with it. The financial benefits of sticking to a budget that you've customized for your own personal situation will grow larger and larger with time.

There is a sort of snowball effect: It starts small, with merely not living paycheck to paycheck, then you start to reach another goal, and then a bigger one, and an even bigger one after that.

Imagine you pay off your first credit card in full. This frees up money that you can use to pay off your car faster. Then once that's done you have even more money that can be used to pay off the rest of your debt. And then once you are no longer a slave to high interest on your debts, you have even more money that you can now put towards something fun, like a vacation. And after that, maybe you'll save up for a house. Or maybe you'll start to put aside money to save for retirement. And on it goes.

The goals will change from person to person, but the principle remains the same. The longer you stick with this, the greater the rewards, and the easier it will be to keep up the motivation you need to stick with your plan.

So give this a good chance to work, and then enjoy the well-deserved successes and triumphs that come your way!

Coming Up

I added the next chapter to this second edition to address false beliefs about money and happiness that can hold you back from achieving your goal of taking control of your money. Read it and find out the real truth about money and happiness, along with the studies to back it up.

The Big Lie About Money and Happiness

Wealth is the ability to fully experience life. Henry David Thoreau

For a lot of people, false beliefs about money and happiness sabotage their efforts to create a life where they always have enough of it.

And I don't want that to happen to you.

For example...

Have you ever heard the platitude that "Money can't buy happiness?"

Well, that's a perfect example of the kind of nonsense I'm talking about.

That popular saying makes it sound as if having more money will never do anything to make a person happier by improving one's life satisfaction, lowering stress, or allowing one to afford to do fun things that add happiness to one's life. So why bother paying much attention to it.

When in truth, depending on the circumstances, having more money can do all of the above.

Let me explain.

First, remember that I'm certainly not saying that money can *always* buy happiness. Nor am I saying that all fun things in life cost money. Because as with most things in life, there are caveats, layers of grey, and all that.

But you, dear reader, are smart enough to know that, right?

If you agree with me that money has the potential to increase your happiness, then keep reading and find out exactly how it can do that.

And if you're a giant skeptic, if you're sure that money can never, ever buy happiness, then please at least give me the benefit of the doubt for the few minutes it'll take you to read this chapter.

Because this knowledge just might give you a bit more motivation to try that much harder to take control of your money once and for all, to ensure that you always have enough of it.

Ending your stressful paycheck-to-paycheck lifestyle will not only allow you to stretch your money further, but by preventing yourself from running out of money, by ensuring that you always have enough of it, I dare say you'll end up less stressed and more satisfied with your life overall.

The thing that kills me about the nonsense of "money doesn't buy happiness" is that it's too often used as a cop out to encourage people to accept their paycheck-to-paycheck struggle-filled existence without question. Because if money can't buy happiness, then why try to make your money go further? Or, to put it another way, why bother trying to improve your financial situation at all if you won't be any happier for it?

So here's why money CAN buy happiness (and I'm going to show you the studies to prove it, albeit with a few caveats, as I mentioned earlier).

First, I'm going to start with some common sense.

Imagine this scenario.

You're homeless, you have no job, and to get something to eat you have to search through the trash to find scraps of food (or beg, or go to soup kitchens). No-one will hire you for a job because you look shabby and unkept (heck, you have nowhere to shower, so you can't help it).

Are you happy?

Probably not.

Now imagine this.

By some enormous stroke of luck, a rich good Samaritan tells you they'll give you enough money to cover the rent for a decent apartment, the cost of groceries, the cost of a decent wardrobe, and the cost of utilities.

Did this windfall bring you some measure of happiness and a feeling of well-being?

I bet the answer is yes. Having the money to pay for basic necessities will do that for a person, won't it. Money just bought some happiness, my friend.

Now obviously you can't depend on luck to pay for your living expenses, so you're going to have to take care of yourself.

But the point is that if you're in the unfortunate situation (like many people) of struggling to pay your bills, worrying about how you'd survive if you lost your job, and you don't have enough cash set aside to pay for emergency expenses, not having enough money is causing unhappiness and stress.

If you fix all that, the odds are high that you'll be happier overall. Period.

The Proof

A recent study[4] in the *Journal of Personality and Social Psychology* looked into the reasons why a higher income is associated with happiness, and found that income was a predictor of one's life evaluation. More income meant being able to afford a better standard of living, which presumably increased one's life evaluation.

Another study[5], co-authored by Nobel Prize winner Angus Deaton, and quoted in a wide range of publications including Time, Forbes, and even The Wall Street Journal, found that "less money is associated with emotional pain". It also found that on average, emotional well-being increased as income did, up to the point where people were making $75,000 per year.

But. It's important to remember that $75,000 was an *average* figure. If you live in an area with an extremely expensive cost of living, that number will be higher. If you live in an area with a low cost of living, that figure will be lower. Got it?

Another key takeaway from the Deaton study is that if a person makes even more money, beyond that $75,000 threshold, happiness does NOT necessarily decrease.

So you don't have to worry about feeling horribly depressed if you get rich, live in a mansion, plus own a yacht and private jet. Sure, your life will be more complicated in some ways, but apparently the extra money will help to negate the downsides of that and your happiness level is likely to remain stable.

Greater Life Satisfaction and Less Emotional Pain

So I don't know about you, but to me, the increase in life satisfaction and decrease in emotional pain that tends to come with having enough money sounds better than the alternative.

Just because a lot of people fall prey to overly simplistic platitudes that discourage improving one's financial situation doesn't mean that you have to.

Ignore it when you hear or read things like, "Money is the root of all evil," and the one that I mentioned at the start of this chapter, "Money doesn't buy happiness." You know better than that.

And if the idea of having more money makes you feel guilty, because you see people around you who don't have enough, then this next section is a must-read.

Buy Happiness for Others?

Remember this. Once you have enough money to pay your bills, a healthy emergency fund, a solid plan for building a retirement nest egg, and no longer worry about running out of money, you can turn your attention to doing good with the money you have.

Because if you're broke, it's not possible to donate to people and charities that you care about, it's not possible to give your children the kind of life they deserve, and it's not possible to give yourself the kind of life that YOU deserve.

But when you finally take charge of your money, you can do all that and more.

- You can help someone in need with their medical expenses.
- You can donate to charities that you believe in and other good causes.
- If you have young children, you can fund their participation in sports, music, or other lessons.
- You can help your older children with the expense of going to college. You can fund your own continuing education.

There are endless possibilities for doing good with your money.

Obviously I can't promise that you'll end up the richest person in America[6], like Bill Gates.

And there are a ton of other things in life, besides money, that will contribute to your happiness, or lack thereof.

But if you stick with the process of using the Money Tracker to take charge of your finances, I can promise you a more secure financial future, a lot less stress, more satisfaction with your life, and yes, even the opportunity to buy a little bit of happiness for others by helping them with their struggles as you see fit.

Next Steps

There's no better time than now to get started in controlling your money. If you haven't done so already, now is the time to go back to the beginning of the chapter titled "Budgeting 101: How to Make a Budget" and work through the steps that I explain there. The main purpose of that chapter is to familiarize yourself with the Money Tracker and how it works. Don't rush it, take your time, and you will get to the end, I promise.

Next, go through the steps in the chapter titled "Month 1: Find Out Where You Stand". Don't let yourself get overwhelmed by the task ahead of you — if you patiently work through that chapter step-by-step, you'll get it all done.

Continue to do as instructed in that chapter over your first month. At the end of your first month, go on to the chapter titled "Month 2: This is the Part Where You Take Control of Your Money" and follow the instructions there.

At the end of your second month of your journey to take control of your money, go to the chapter titled "Month 3 and Beyond: How to Stay on Track".

If you need an extra dose of motivation, reminders about why you're doing this in the first place, or tips for saving money, come back to the book and re-read the chapters on those topics.

Did You Enjoy This Book?

I want to thank you for purchasing and reading this book. I really hope you got a lot out of it!

Can I ask you for a quick favor though?

If you enjoyed this book, I would really appreciate it if you could leave me a review on Amazon.

I love getting feedback from my readers, and reviews on Amazon really do make a difference. I read all of my reviews and would really love to hear your thoughts.

Thanks so much!

Avery Breyer

P.S. You can click here to go directly to the book on Amazon and leave your review.

Thank-You For Reading My Book!

If you haven't done so already, please accept **my FREE special report, How to Save Money When You Don't Have Any.** It's my way of thanking you for downloading my book!

I think you'll find it interesting — it contains a really simple savings strategy that most people overlook.

I'd also like to give you **a FREE copy of the Money Tracker.** It will be much easier for you to implement the strategies in this book if you use this tool. Rather than wasting time trying to make a spreadsheet yourself, you can just take this one out of its virtual box and use it immediately! It's an insanely useful tool that I've used for years to keep an eye on my budget, and I know you'll love it!

Get it all here:

https://averybreyer.com/1hr-budget-how-to-stop-living-paycheck-to-paycheck-opt-in/

More Books By Avery Breyer

How to Raise Your Credit Score

A high credit score makes it easier to get approved for renting a home or apartment, getting a mortgage to buy a home, getting that credit card with the nice bonuses, and so much more. Find out how to make the most of your score with the simple, easy-to-implement strategies laid out in this book.

How to Be Debt Free

Debt is one of the biggest problems plaguing the middle class and can be a massive road block to building wealth for you and your family. Get out of debt and stay debt-free forever with this simple, time-tested, step-by-step plan that anyone can follow! (Formerly published as *Your Road to Wealth Starts Here*.)

Turn Your Computer Into a Money Machine

This no BS book describes the exact method I used to start up a lucrative side hustle that earned me as much as $60 per hour, despite starting out with no experience, no credentials, and no contacts. Important: this is not some pie-in-the-sky, passive income "get rich quick" scheme, so if that's what you're looking for, this won't be for you.

(Books are available on Amazon.)

Recommended Reading

This book was meant to be tightly focused on budgeting. But once you master that, you need to figure out how to invest your money for the future.

Here are some books about investing that will give you some ideas:

MONEY Master the Game: 7 Simple Steps to Financial Freedom, by Tony Robbins

Jim Cramer's Get Rich Carefully, by James J. Cramer

And last, but not least…

I don't know about you, but whenever I'm trying to learn a new skill, I like to read the opinions of multiple people.

No matter how good, or how complete a book is, I find that I always pick up at least one new insight or trick from every NEW book I read on a topic of interest to me.

So, without further ado, here are some other budgeting and general money management books that I think you'll find helpful:

The Total Money Makeover, by Dave Ramsey

The Money Book for the Young, Fabulous and Broke, by Suze Orman

Rich Dad Poor Dad, by Robert T. Kiyosaki

The Richest Man in Babylon, by George S. Clason

The Millionaire Next Door, by Thomas J. Stanley Ph.D.

1. http://www.mindsetonline.com/whatisit/
whatdoesthismeanforme/
2. Implementation Intentions and the Theory of Planned Behavior,
Personality and Social Psychology Bulletin September 1997,vol. 23,
no. 9, 945-954
3. Good intentions, bad habits, and effects of forming implementation
intentions on healthy eatingEuropean Journal of Social Psychology,
vol. 29, no. 5-6, pp. 591-604, 1999
4. Wealth and happiness across the world: material prosperity
predicts life evaluation, whereas psychosocial prosperity predicts
positive feeling. Journal of Personality and Social Psychology, 2010
Jul; vol. 99(1):52-61
5. High income improves evaluation of life but not emotional well-
being. Proceedings of the National Academy of Sciences of the
United States of America, 2010 Aug 4, vol. 107, no. 38,
16489-16493
6. http://www.forbes.com/forbes-400/

Made in the USA
Middletown, DE
06 November 2023